# What's the Point of Political Philosophy?

# What's the Point of Political Philosophy?

Jonathan Floyd

polity

First published in 2019 by Polity Press

Polity Press
65 Bridge Street
Cambridge CB2 1UR, UK

Polity Press
101 Station Landing
Suite 300
Medford, MA 02155, USA

ISBN-13: 978-1-5095-2418-1
ISBN-13: 978-1-5095-2419-8 (pb)

A catalogue record for this book is available from the British Library.

Library of Congress Cataloging-in-Publication Data

Names: Floyd, Jonathan, 1980- author.
Title: What's the point of political philosophy? / Jonathan Floyd.
Other titles: What is the point of political philosophy?
Description: Medford, Massachusetts : Polity, 2019. | Includes
    bibliographical references and index.
Identifiers: LCCN 2018053019 (print) | LCCN 2019008913 (ebook) | ISBN
    9781509524228 (Epub) | ISBN 9781509524181 | ISBN 9781509524181(Hardback)
    | ISBN 9781509524198(Paperback)
Subjects: LCSH: Political science--Philosophy.
Classification: LCC JA71 (ebook) | LCC JA71 .F566 2019 (print) | DDC
    320.01--dc23
LC record available at https://lccn.loc.gov/2018053019

Typeset in 11 on 14 pt Sabon by Servis Filmsetting Ltd, Stockport, Cheshire
Printed and bound in Great Britain by CPI Group (UK) Ltd, Croydon

For further information on Polity, visit our website: politybooks.com

# Contents

# Acknowledgements

Thanks are due here in at least five different directions. First, for advice, my editor George Owers, together with the reviewers he engaged on our behalf. George has been, at all times in this process, an informed and involved presence, for which I am very grateful indeed. Second, for helpful conversations and numerous teas and coffees, my wife. This is neither the first nor the last book of mine she has helped me through. Third, for inspiration, my children. Generally, they distract me from work yet all the while imbue it with more meaning than it could otherwise have. Fourth, for support, my department here in Bristol. This book would not have been completed without the well-timed term of study leave they provided. Fifth, for the feedback they didn't realise they were giving, my marvellous Bristol students. Sharp as tacks and ambitious as lions, yet also friendly and curious, each generation of undergraduates here in 'SPAIS' has been a pleasure to teach, and I have more faith in that trend continuing than just about any other in the modern world.

# Foreword

Fascists burn books for the same reason philosophers write them – they matter. They matter because they change how people think and, in turn, how they behave. They matter because they can preserve politics as it is or turn it on its head. They matter because, if they are not burnt, they sometimes start fires all of their own. None of which, of course, means that all books are equally incendiary. Most, including this one, are neither spark nor kindling and aim only, as I do, for light rather than heat. If, by the end of these chapters, I have simply left you keen to read more political philosophy – if I have left you interested, rather than inflamed – then I shall be a happy author. And yet, if you are thinking of setting the world alight, it wouldn't be the worst idea to start here. Although I won't tell you what to think about revolutions, constitutions, and the fine line between utopia and dystopia, I might be able to tell you something of *how* to think about such things.

# 1
# Introduction

## 1.1 What's the point of it all?

We start here with a question. If you ask a political philosopher what the point is of their subject, what do you think they would say? The truth is, you wouldn't get an answer at all, given the way that they – or indeed *we* – normally carry on. Instead, you would probably end up being asked a question yourself, and normally one along the lines of 'Well, what do you mean by *point*?' To this you should say nothing, because, if you are lucky, they might elaborate by saying something like: 'Well, do you mean the *motive* of the person doing it?' For example, I do it to make me happy. Do you mean their *intention*? For example, I do it to change the world. Or do you mean the immediate *objective* of whatever it is they are working on? For example, I'm currently analysing the concept of freedom in order better to understand what freedom is, despite fearing this won't change the world, and despite getting rather unhappy about that very fear. After such elaboration, their demeanour will vary according to age. If they are old, they will lean back, pleased with their efforts, as smug as a swan. If they are young, they will lean in, unintendedly aggressive, ready to defend their uses of terms such as motive and intention and impatient for the next chance to hear themselves think.

What can one learn from this *almost* imaginary exchange? First, we learn straight away that there are clearly going to be *many* points to political philosophy in the sense of the various ends it serves, each of which could animate, alone or in combination, whoever it is that is doing or reading it. As with most things in life, we need not pursue it for just *one* reason. Think here, for example, of marriage. Is it about love, sex, family, public celebration and affirmation, companionship, security, or something else altogether? Naturally, for different individuals, and different marriages, all sorts of reasons, and various combinations of reasons, will apply. Second, we learn a little less quickly that part of the point of political philosophy, and a part that has very much to do with the 'philosophy' half of it, is of course to *think about* its very point. 'What is the point of political philosophy?', after all, is a very philosophical question, as is 'What is a point?', 'What is the point of thinking about points?', and, naturally, 'What is the point of thinking about thinking about points?'

Before we indulge ourselves, however, let's now get much more to the point and focus specifically on *this* book and *political* philosophy. What, exactly, are my key claims here? What precisely is – or *are* – the point – or *points* – of this subject? Well, as explained by chapter 2, at one level the point of political philosophy is to tell us not how politics worked in the *past*, or how it works in the *present*, but how it should work in the *future*. If somebody asked you *what* political philosophy is, you could answer with that mission. Then, at a second level, and as explained by chapter 3, its point is to *analyse* our key political ideas, *critique* them, and figure out how they could be *ordered* into some ideal and organising vision. If somebody asked you *how* to do political philosophy, you could answer with that list of three tasks. Then, at a third level, as shown by chapter 4, its point is to *guide* individuals and societies, helping them to figure out what they should think about both the status quo and its alternatives. If somebody asked you *why* you teach, publish, and discuss political philosophy, as opposed to just keeping it to yourself, you could answer with that ambition. And again, at a fourth level, and as shown by all three of these chapters, a further point of political philosophy is also to *reflect upon these very points*, if only in order to check that we got those first three levels right. If, therefore, somebody asks *you* why you're writing a book called 'What's the Point of Political Philosophy?', then that point, I would suggest, should be part of your answer.

Now, in order to be as clear as possible, we can also put these same points in a different order. Let's say, for example, that you ask a political philosopher what they are thinking about, and they say 'the nature of freedom (or justice, or legitimacy, or whatever)'. To this you might say, especially if you are rude, 'But what's the point of that?' They then reply that it's important to *analyse*, *critique*, and *order* our key political ideas. You then say: 'But what's the point of that?' They then reply that we need to get a handle on such things in order to know how politics *should* be organised, as opposed to just how it's organised *right now*. You then say: 'But what's the point of that?' They then reply that when they *publish* such work, and their colleagues publish similar work, and when we all *talk* about it and *teach* it, then together we weave a tapestry that society can draw upon when faced with inevitable and difficult choices about how to organise itself. And then? At this point, I would hope, you let them get on with what they were doing.

There is, though, a further question here regarding what exactly I am trying to achieve with this book by explaining these various 'points' to political philosophy. The answer to that is simple. My aim is to provide an original but accessible account of our subject – my subject – political philosophy. Or, more precisely, I want to tell readers what political philosophy *is*, how you can *do* it, and why you might *want* to do it. Yet what, you might say – for that is the kind of person you've become – is the real *point* of that?

We can think about that question from the point of view of three groups of readers. First, for *scholars*, the point of this book is to push forward our understanding of the nature, methods, and purposes of our field, thus giving them something new, and hopefully nutritious, into which to dig their critical teeth. There are many of us today interested in the practice and purpose of our subject, whether working on 'realism' vs. 'moralism',[1] 'ideal' vs. 'non-ideal' theory,[2] 'transcendental' vs. 'comparative' theory,[3] 'political political theory',[4] or something else altogether,[5] and for such people I hope the book will be a welcome, and short, addition to their reading lists. Second, for *students*, the point is to guide them through a subject to which they might be new or in which they now need more detailed methodological advice, perhaps in the pursuit of an essay, a dissertation, or a doctoral thesis. Third, for *members of the general public*, assuming any such wonderful creatures ever read this book, the point is to tell them not just what our subject involves but also why it matters, in the various ways that it does. Yet presumably, if you've paid for this book, you already have some inkling of this, unless of course you're just skim-reading via Google, in which case you certainly haven't paid for anything.

At this point I imagine you have just one final and fundamental question to ask, namely: Who exactly am *I* to be writing this? I would expect you to ask that question, given your form so far, although you might, to be fair, phrase it somewhat more precisely and politely. You might, for example, say something like this: How exactly does what I've been working on for the last decade or so feed into this book? Surely, though, the answer is clear? *Obviously* I'm a *fox* who's turning into a *hedgehog*. Or, if that's not so clear, let me explain. In philosophical circles these days, a hedgehog is someone who knows one big thing, while a fox knows lots of little things.[6] That is, a hedgehog is someone who, at least over time, ends up sitting on one big and important truth, while foxes run around sniffing out and digging up all sorts of smaller ones. Why then am I becoming a hedgehog? Well, because initially in my career I *was* interested in all sorts of things. I was interested in what, if anything, political philosophy needed to take on board from history.[7] I was interested in whether political philosophy needs to be more realistic and less utopian.[8] I was interested in the dense systems of thought built

5

up by the likes of John Rawls and Joseph Raz.[9] All of which, you might think, is very fox-like behaviour. Yet really I was a hedgehog on the make, because all of this work, in essence, was focused on the key points discussed so far – regarding what political philosophy is, how it can be done, and why we might want to do it. At all times, you might say, I was interested in the nature, methods, and purposes of our subject. This is why, a couple of years ago, I wrote a long book called *Is Political Philosophy Impossible?*,[10] but also why, today, I'm writing this rather shorter one. This, after all, is a book designed for both the new and the established and for both the methodologically minded – interested in the same *meta*-issues as me – and those more conventionally inclined – interested in the kind of analysis, critique, and ordering touched on above, as well as the political guidance to which it can lead.

## 1.2 Three chapter overviews

How then, exactly, is the book organised? The structure is simple. As touched on above, there are three chapters on three topics, each of which covers something different you might have in mind when asking what the point is of political philosophy. The first of these explains what political philosophy *is*, expanding on the idea that our mission is to figure out not how politics is or has been organised, but how it *should* be organised. The second then explains how to do political philosophy, expanding on the idea that our three core objectives are to analyse, critique, and order our key political ideas. The third, finally, explains what the wider benefits of this work are, expanding on the idea that, by pursuing these objectives, we are providing something that helps society through all sorts of tricky political choices.

These three treatments, to give a little more depth here, go roughly as follows. First, in chapter 2, in order to explain what political philosophy is, I start off by reviewing the various ways in which other people have tried to define political philosophy and end up arguing that the best way to define it is in terms of what I call its 'organising question', namely, 'How should we live?' This question is closely related to the question I have mentioned twice already as a good way into the topic – 'What should politics be like?' – yet has the added benefit that it does not assume in advance that we should have *any* politics at all. One might, after all, be a certain kind of anarchist or want to be jettisoned off into space, floating around in a fibreglass pod with no interaction with other human beings. Unlikely, you might think, but not impossible. This 'organising question', as you will see, becomes important when it comes to making sense of certain things that follow later.

Next up, in chapter 3, I argue that there are, as noted, three tasks one might want to perform when trying to answer that question. These, once more, are *analysis*, *critique*, and *ordering*. The first, analysis, involves dissecting and illuminating the key ideas at stake in politics – variables we want to control, such as power and equality, and problems we want to avoid, such as exploitation and domination. The second, critique, involves knocking down some of these ideas, or at least qualifying their appeal. We might, for example, be less enamoured of equality if it involves levelling down the special to the height of the ordinary, just as we might be less enamoured of liberty if it means a great time for the wolves and not such a great time for the sheep. The third, ordering, involves arguing for a particular set of principles which, when put together, would *define* a particular political order, such as liberal democracy. In doing so, it would also be telling us not just which variables and problems to focus upon but also how to prioritise among them when not all good things can be had to the same extent. We might, for example, think both that free speech is desirable *and* that so-called hate speech is undesirable, but end up choosing a political order that protects the first even when it permits the second.

Finally, chapter 4 discusses some of the wider purposes one might have in mind when doing political philosophy, focusing in particular on the kind of guidance mentioned already, but dividing that guidance into the two goals of *orientating individuals* and *benefiting societies*. Regarding the first, orientating individuals, political philosophy offers the promise of helping you or me figure out just what we should think of the political world in which we live and what a better alternative might look like, if indeed there is one. Regarding the second, benefiting societies, it offers the promise of helping them move forward, by setting out new ideas for us to discuss, inoculating against bad ideas, and guiding both politicians and the general mass of voters on both fronts. Here we have a vision of the political philosopher as, on different occasions, the sage on stage, the guide by the side, but also the crank in the cupboard (or office, depending on status) to whom you go with an essay plan. The last of these might not seem like a role with particularly wide-reaching ramifications, but – who knows? – just sometimes our students go on to change the world, even if their tutors, at least directly, do not.

## 1.3 A bit of pushback

There's now just one last 'point' to make in this introduction. Bearing in mind here my claim that part of the point of political philosophy, as noted, is to change the world, one might wonder at this juncture whether *this* book really has anything to do with *that* ambition. Well, the reality, to be blunt, is that it doesn't, unless it is read either by vast numbers of people or by just a few people with vast influence, neither of which is very likely. Nonetheless, assuming the possibility of just something along these lines, however small the scale, I will say just a few words about a current of opinion I'm keen to push back against in what follows, and especially when it comes to the final chapter. This is a current of opinion – the contemporary public climate of opinion – in which political philosophy plays almost no *visible* role. This is not to say that it plays no role whatsoever – as explained in chapter 4, political philosophy already shapes the world in more ways than we notice – but, all the same, what it does not do is play a role in the wider public imagination, in the sense that most people have heard neither of political philosophy nor of any individual political philosophers. As you will see, this is something I want to alter.

Why, though, should that *matter*? Why would one need to *change* that? Well, consider here that, as things stand, and despite the current climate of 'anti-expertise' in Western politics, we still go to doctors for our health, to mechanics for our cars, to architects for our buildings, and so on and so forth. We still, that is, rely on experts, even while disparaging them in general. As a result, we might wonder – to whom exactly do we go for our *politics*? Whom do we call when *that* needs fixing or improving? Politicians, you might suppose, though we say we don't trust them,[11] and it's not clear exactly what expertise they have besides experience of the job itself.[12] Gurus and columnists then, or maybe think tanks, even if, again, it's not always obvious what grasp they have either of the key political ideas currently in play or of the options we might have for changing them. They might, of course, know about focus-group polling, data analytics, campaign strategies, economic modelling, and even the empirical evaluation of existing policies, in the sense of working out what causes what and whether stated aims matched up to observed outcomes. But what about, say, *equality, freedom, justice, legitimacy*? What about the core ideas at the heart of our rhetoric, our passions, and our key political choices?

These ideas, as we know, are the key terms that get bandied about in every speech, pamphlet, manifesto, and tweet – yet what exactly do politicians and voters know of their nature and importance? What do they know of the ways in which they can and can't be moulded and traded off against each other? Of the hope and danger they contain? What do they know, to give just one recent and close-to-home example, of their place in the debate over Britain's membership of the European Union? In that question, like so many political questions, we had to think about the nature of democracy, legitimacy, community, freedom, and so on, yet there was clearly no real grasp, wherever you looked, of any such things. People on both sides simply used terms as they saw fit to use them, and nobody, at least in mainstream debate, got to the heart of the matter. Just as we saw in the same country in the previous year, this time on the question of Scottish independence, one side thought it self-evident that being ruled closer to home was better than being ruled from further away – though if London trumps Brussels, and Edinburgh trumps London, wouldn't Aberdeen trump Edinburgh? The other side, in turn, just took it for granted that economic growth was what really mattered, and they did so, for the most part, regardless of how it would be supplied and distributed, and regardless of the competence or impartiality of those who predicted it.

None of which, of course, means that political philosophers are the ghostbusters you didn't know you could call upon, and it would be disastrous if political philosophers, myself included, thought that themselves. We are not some strange breed of underpaid consultants, waiting for the bat-signal of a referendum or election, or even just a phone call from someone we used to know but whom now almost everyone knows. The key point here is about the wider understanding of key political ideas that exists, or does not exist, in society as a whole. Surely, I would suggest, we would do better if our politicians were experts in such things; surely, I would infer, we would be more likely to get such politicians if society at large had a better handle on them. On this front, I think, Plato was on to something when he wrote that politics will never be what it ought to be unless either philosophers become kings (or queens) or kings (or queens) become philosophers. Of course, nobody today wants kings (or queens) any more, philosophical or otherwise, but there is truth in what he says. Clearly, we like the idea of our politicians being *wise* in some way or other, and we reprimand them all the time when we think they fall short in that department. We don't want them to be incompetent or lacking direction, and we'd like it very much indeed if they really *knew* what a better political world would be, and how we might get there. Yet what can we do about that?

Now, what you might well be thinking at this point, perfectly reasonably, is that writing a book such as this one, for the probably-already-interested, is not much of a solution. The arguments that follow, we assume, are likely to reach only those who already have some interest in the subject, meaning that, despite my best efforts, I'm really just preaching to the choir. So what exactly am I trying to say here? What exactly do I hope for, if anything, beyond the core goals, and for readers of this book, as set out above? Well, following Plato's worry about philosophy and political wisdom, we might also note here that, more than two thousand years later, a deep worry for the nineteenth century, facing the prospect of expanding democratic suffrage, was that mass democracy in an uneducated society would lead to the 'tyranny of the majority'. And, again, there's clearly truth in that worry too, as shown by the events of the mid-twentieth century. Yet that does not mean we have to be *elitists* or that our only option is to *limit* democracy, as many in the nineteenth and twentieth centuries believed. After all, hemming democracy in with legal checks and balances, devolution and federalism, and the selfish flows of global capitalism might only add to the instability we fear. Instead, I want to suggest, we have another option, and one which would bring political philosophy right into play. This is the option we never think about: the option of changing, not the system – *cracy* – but the people – *demos*. If we could change *them*, and this is where my book comes in, we could change politics at a fundamental level. We would be changing the citizens and, in turn, the politicians, all of whom would now be held accountable by a new generation of voters, to whom in turn they could speak in new and enriched ways.

Let me explain this idea. Imagine, if you will, a world in which political philosophy was taught, at least to some extent, to, say, sixteen-year-olds, just two years before they become voters in most democracies. Imagine them then understanding the key ideas at stake in our major political decisions and having a vocabulary to match. And note, in imagining this world, you should not be imagining one in which teenagers are taught *what to think* about each issue. The focus is simply on *how to think* about our key political ideas. Rather than indoctrinating anyone, we would simply be sharing ideas and arguments, on either side of every issue, with those to whom the big political decisions will, in the long run, matter the most. Or, put differently, we would simply be teaching political philosophy in schools in much the same way we already teach it at universities – except that now we would be doing it with everyone rather than just the self-selected. At all times, of course, it would be up to them to decide what to make of it all, just as it is always up to them whom to vote for, and indeed whether or not to vote. Yet we would have expanded their imagination while refining their judgement. With the right philosophical background, not only could citizens choose in wiser ways, they would also end up with more options to choose from.

## Introduction

The aim I have in mind here, then, is enlightenment rather than conversion, though I suppose that still leaves unclear the question of where exactly this book fits into it all. After all, does this book cover all, or even most, of the material required for such teaching? Does it transform the public status of political philosophy and transform the very *demos* on which every democracy depends? Does it reach the many rather than the few? Well, clearly not, on all fronts. It can only ever be just a drop in the ocean, and my hope is simply that the few this book reaches somehow have more ability than I do to reach the many in the way I've sketched out. There is, though, a further important point buried here regarding this book and its topic, and which required this wider discussion of the place of political philosophy in contemporary society – namely, that the extent to which political philosophy *matters* is in part bound up with the extent to which a society *already* understands it, accesses it, and does it. There's more *point*, after all, to research on power stations if you live in a country with electricity, just as there's more *point* to political philosophy if you live in a country that knows what it is. Political philosophy has more 'point', in other words, when more people are aware of it. I just hope that, in time, this 'drop in the ocean' becomes something like a drop of purple dye in clear water or, better yet, a drop of blood in a sea of sharks. Of course we know that most people, for now, will know nothing of this book or the subject it discusses – but that is only for now. In the future, perhaps just a few influential individuals will give this subject of ours even more 'point' than it has at present.

# 2
# What?

## 2.1 Introduction

This chapter provides a new and hopefully helpful way of defining political philosophy, after first working through a critical discussion of the different ways in which others have defined it. This discussion is something you won't find in otherwise excellent overviews of our subject, given the usual practice of authors defining it as they see fit before quickly moving on to a survey of the arguments the subject contains – about justice, rights, freedom, and so on. It's also something that would be unnecessary in many other subjects in which the reader might be interested. Consider, for example, that we do not normally struggle to define a table, a planet, or a bird. Of course, sometimes items fall in and out of those categories – Pluto was, but is now no longer, a planet – and sometimes definitions are split into two or more pieces – birds that used to be called marsh tits are now divided into two species, willow tits and marsh tits.

Most of the time, however, scholars agree on these definitions, and on what falls in and outside of them, to an extent that political philosophers have yet to manage. Our task here is to try and improve on that situation.

## 2.2 A working definition

So: political philosophy is an academic subject. Simple. Political philosophy is an academic subject normally found in philosophy departments and politics departments.[1] Simple again. Political philosophy is a subject that is sometimes called 'political philosophy' and sometimes 'political theory', with the best rule of thumb being that it tends to be called the former in philosophy departments and the latter in politics departments.[2] Strange, but again simple. Political philosophy is a subject concerned with … what? This is the big question, and the simplest answer to it is this: political philosophy is a subject concerned not with what politics is like right now, or what it was like in the past, but rather with what it *should* be like in the future.

This topic – what politics *should* be like – gives us a pretty good working definition for now, and also one that you could use for the rest of this book if you want to skip ahead. It also gives us a definition that chimes with several accounts offered by others. For example, Strauss describes political philosophy as 'the attempt truly to know both the nature of political things and the right, or the good, political order'.[3] Scanlon describes it as focused on the 'standards by which political, legal, and economic institutions should be assessed'.[4] Matravers describes it as concerned with 'what political practices and institutions are justified and ought to be established'.[5] McAfee describes it as a 'field for developing new ideals, practices, and justifications for how political institutions and practices should be organised and reconstructed'.[6] In all four cases, the key idea is the same. What we have here, they agree, is a subject concerned with what the political world *should* or *ought to* be like.

What we are *not* interested in, then, is explaining the start of the Cold War or understanding how voting worked in the Roman Republic. We are not interested in comparing the 2015 UK general election with the 2017 UK general election. We are not interested in predicting future conflicts, elections, or voting innovations. Understanding, explanation, comparison, prediction – these are not our primary business. We are interested, by contrast, in *pre*scription and *pro*scription – what should and should not be the case in the world, and in particular what should and should not be the case in politics. You want to change the world? You want to know what a better one would look like? Then this is your field.

### 2.3 Digging deeper – concepts and institutions

Saying that political philosophy is about 'what politics should be like', however, only gives us a 'working definition', as noted. This is because it rather begs the question of what politics *is*. Are we interested, for example, in international politics, electoral politics, or the politics of the family? Yet perhaps that is not too much of a problem. We might, after all, simply defer the issue via the following three-stage argument. First, a premise: politics is an artificial practice. Unlike the formation of clouds or the movement of planets, it is something created and run by us. That is an important truth for political philosophy, just as it is for the distinction between the natural and human sciences more generally. Atoms, for example, do not start revolutions after reading *The Communist Manifesto*. Second, a deduction: if it's created and run by us, then it's also up to us what form it takes. We can make it local or global, familial or impersonal, as we see fit. Third, a further deduction: if it's up to us what form it takes, then it must be the job of political philosophy to advise us on this form, meaning that the term 'politics' just can't be decided in advance.

All of this, I think, is perfectly sensible, but also misleading. Consider, for example, that if I gave you a recipe for chicken vindaloo, I couldn't just say, well, it's up to *me* what politics is, and on my view it's all about curry. Clearly, we can't all just make up our own definitions of politics. Clearly, we all have some shared criteria in mind when discussing it. Clearly, we can be more specific than this and provide some limits as to what 'counts' as politics. Clearly – but how?

Here are two options. First, we might limit our subject by focusing it on a concept more specific than 'politics'. Rawls, for example, suggests something like this when declaring that 'justice' is the first virtue of political institutions.[7] Berlin, similarly, says on one occasion that political philosophy is about the 'ends of life'[8] and on another that it's about 'men's relationships to each other and to their institutions'.[9] Blackburn, sticking with the relationship theme, defines it in terms of 'relations between the collective and the individual'.[10] Bevir, agreeing with 'collective', talks of 'public affairs and collective decision making'.[11] Williams, breaking with both of them, says that political philosophy centres on 'distinctively political concepts', such as 'power' and 'legitimation'.[12] Goodwin, sharing Williams's 'power' theme, writes that 'political theory [can] be defined as the discipline which aims to explain, justify or criticise the disposition of power in society.'[13] So, in each of these six cases we have some further concept with which to make sense of politics and thus political philosophy – whether that be justice, power, legitimacy, relationships between the collective and the individual, or even the 'ends of life'. Call these the *conceptual* approaches to defining political philosophy.

Now our second option. This approach makes sense of our subject by focusing it not on an abstract concept, such as justice or power, but on concrete institutions observable in the real world. Consider five examples this time. First, Swift, who writes that political philosophy is about 'what the state ought (and ought not) to do'.[14] Second, Nozick, who claims that it is about 'how the state should be organised' and, even more fundamentally, about 'whether there should be any state at all'.[15] Third, Plamenatz, who defines it in terms of 'systematic thinking about the purposes of government'.[16] Fourth, Miller, who describes it as 'an investigation into the nature, causes, and effects of good and bad government'.[17] Fifth, Pettit, who equates it with the evaluation of *both* government and state.[18] So, what we have here are five thinkers and, as it happens, just two institutions: *state* and *government*. Call these the *institutional* approaches.

What should we think about these two options? A first thought is that the line between them is rather blurry. We might say, for example, that political philosophy is concerned chiefly with the concept of *legitimacy*, and that legitimacy is about who should have *power* over whom. Or we might say that political philosophy is about the *state*, with the state defined as a body that organises the distribution of *power*. At this point it becomes clear that we could be doing one and the same subject, whether we started with an abstract concept, such as legitimacy, dreamed up from our armchair, or a concrete institution, such as the state, sat in front of us. Or is that too simple? After all, how would we know what *counts* as a state in our world unless we had some concept in mind that told us as much? If that's right, then concepts must come first and are the real roots of our definitions. Or, on the other hand, we might alternatively wonder how we could have a concept of the state unless we'd *already* seen or *read* about one. Nobody had a concept of tennis five hundred years ago, or Facebook fifty years ago, so how could one grasp political institutions, such as the state, before they had been invented? So, if *that's* right, then institutions must be fundamental, and our concepts, however general and timeless they might seem, are simply *abstractions* from the world as we know it.

Clearly, we are in tricky territory here, which is why it might be helpful to come at this puzzle from a different angle. Consider, therefore, a further definition offered by Wolff. He writes that political philosophy is about the distribution of goods (who gets what?) and the distribution of power (says who?).[19] This seems like a pretty handy definition of political philosophy, though the question it raises is obvious: What *kind* of definition is it? A *conceptual* one centred on goods and power – or even on justice (who gets what goods) and legitimacy (who has the power to decide)? Or an *institutional* one, given that Wolff might really be starting here with the question of how existing processes or institutions should operate, meaning in this case something like the economy and the state – two institutions with which we are, of course, abundantly familiar. Once more, it seems as though we could go either way. Perhaps, then, we could say that it depends on what Wolff *has in mind* when invoking these terms – a dreamy concept or a concrete institution. Yet that would be a mistake. It depends more fundamentally on those two problems already noted: (1) Can anyone summon up a political concept without some institution or practice from which it was abstracted?, and (2) Can anyone abstract from an institution or practice without having some prior concept that identifies it?

A further important issue here is that, when contemplating this puzzle, we've also been discussing a blurring of two quite separate domains: the *normative* – how the world should be – and the *descriptive* – how it already is. This is interesting, given what I said earlier about our subject being concerned solely with normative notions of prescription and proscription. Yet consider the following two possibilities. First, you define political philosophy in terms of an existing institution, such as the state, or even something more general, such as 'politics', and then say that its task is to find out not how those things do work but how they *should* work. In this case you've taken what we might call an institutional and normative approach. Second, you define the subject as an enquiry into finding out what justice *is*. Now you're doing something that looks, in contrast, both conceptual and descriptive. *And yet*, if in the first instance you wanted to know how politics should work, while in the second it turns out that justice is – as Rawls suggested – the value that should guide politics, what real difference is there between the two approaches? Surely they're both asking how politics *ought* to be organised? Surely they're both asking what justice *is*? Well, oh dear, you might say, we're in a real muddle now.

## 2.4 Problem-based definitions

In case you've lost count, we've now considered fifteen definitions of our subject, though all we have to show for them, it seems, is a rather stubborn puzzle. Yes, we still have our 'working definition' of political philosophy – it's about what politics should be like in the future – but it's unclear whether we should try and specify the notion of 'politics' in that definition by reference to a further *concept* – such as justice, legitimacy, or power – or some sort of concrete *institution*, such as the state or government.

Let's consider then, as a very different possibility, three ways of defining political philosophy that all describe their subject in terms of specific *problems*, each of which combines *both* concepts and institutions. First, from Cohen, we have the claim that political philosophy is essentially about three things: what justice is, what the state should do, and how social states rank normatively.[20] Second, from Waldron, we have agreement with Cohen on those issues but also the addition of one further problem – that of exactly which institutions we should adopt within whatever counts as a generally just state: First-past-the-post voting? Bicameral legislature? A written constitution? And so on.[21] Third, from Rawls, who earlier talked of justice as 'the first virtue' of political institutions, we again have a claim that there are really four key problems for our subject, though his list differs entirely from Cohen's and Waldron's. These four are as follows:

1 *agreement* – finding a basis for, if not philosophical, at least political agreement between different sides in a divisive moral dispute;
2 *orientation* – helping to place and direct us, in terms of principles, within our own political environment;
3 *reconciliation* – calming our frustrations within the right political order by showing us the rationality of our governing institutions; and
4 *realistic utopia* – probing the limits of practical possibility, which means finding out what a just society would be within unavoidable constraints, including what Rawls calls the 'fact of reasonable pluralism'.[22]

Now, all of these are, I think, promising lists, in the sense that each of them provides an interesting set of tasks around which we could organise our subject. They also, perhaps, solve our nagging problem of whether concepts or institutions are fundamental, if only by seeming to avoid it altogether. They do though bring a new worry, in consequence of that avoidance. When formulating these task lists, how exactly have Cohen, Waldron, and Rawls decided what *counts* as 'in' and 'out'? Or, put differently, what exactly is the rationale behind their selections, and how might we begin to adjudicate between them where they differ?

The answer to that worry, though not obvious from their writings, might become obvious to us if we bring a new idea to the table here: the idea of *interpretation*. This idea helps us in the following way. First, consider here that one could see *all* of these tasks as simply part of a more general task in which political philosophers are involved – the task of taking politics *as it is* and people *as they are* and then seeing what solutions can be worked out for the problems *we already recognise*, bearing in mind the values to which *we already adhere*. On this view, that is, all political philosophers really need to do, in order to frame their subject, is simply *interpret* a particular understanding of politics, including the problems it gives us, from the world as we know it, in the same way we might interpret a lesson or theme from a story, or indeed that politicians interpret the interests and values of their voters. And there's a real pay-off to that move. What it would mean, given the problems discussed, is that we no longer need to worry about where our concepts, institutions, or tasks come from – we simply recognise that they are *ours*, and that they articulate for us a set of problems we *already want to solve*, whether that be, for example, figuring out justice, working out what the state should do, orientating us as individuals, and so on and so forth.

This view, clearly, makes a lot of sense given the discussion so far and also chimes with several approaches we haven't yet covered. Pettit, for example, talks on one occasion of how, in political philosophy, we can work critically with the existing languages of political discussion and legitimation of our time,[23] while Walzer writes that one 'way of doing philosophy is to interpret to one's fellow citizens the world of meanings we share'.[24] James, more recently, advances a 'constructive method' according to which one does political philosophy by understanding and working with the values already present within a particular practice, whether that means modern politics more generally, democracy in particular, or even a specific institution.[25] Or consider Ronald Dworkin. He claims more grandly that the fundamental job of political philosophy is to analyse not just the existing political values of our time but also our wider moral and even aesthetic values in order to find, again, 'interpretations' of them that avoid conflicts with all of the rest.[26]

So, once more, the idea floated here is simply to decide what political philosophy is and does on the basis of the understandings of politics, its problems, and our values *that we already have*. And, once more, the pay-off to that would be that we avoid our concepts/institutions problem by simply starting with the political concepts and institutions that we already have and care about. It doesn't matter, on this view, whether those ideas are based on people coming up with brand new concepts in the past or abstractions from new institutions. All that matters is that there's a group of people, right here and right now, with some shared understanding about politics and also some shared problems resulting from that. A group of people, let's say, who want to agree shared terms of co-operation in light of both their disagreements and their shared values. A group of people, naturally, who need others who can help them understand those disagreements and values. A group of people, we might say, who both need political philosophers and provide the basis for defining political philosophy.

Are we, then, at the end of our quest? Sadly not, if only for the simple reason that this new approach doesn't really put to bed that nagging worry about what's *in* and what's *out*. It is one thing to remark, as Appiah has done when talking about philosophy in general, that the 'best account of disciplinary objects is a historical one', but quite another to decide which bits of that history to accept and reject.[27] What we can't help but wonder, with each attempt at 'interpreting' our subject, is this: Are Pettit, Walzer, James, Dworkin, and so on, identifying the *right* set of problems and values? Are they really speaking for *us*, however big or small, global or national, that 'us' might be? Isn't it all just a bit too *arbitrary*?

Perhaps, though, we could soften this 'arbitrariness' by basing it on many voices rather than just a few. Or, put differently, perhaps we could define our subject collectively rather than individually, making it 'inter-subjective' rather than 'subjective'. This, surely, would make a real difference to our view of these interpreta-tions, just as it makes a difference to our faith in an Olympic diving competition when there are seven judges rather than just one. Consider then here a further group of authors, each of whom, when writing about political philosophy, has chosen to define their subject not just in terms of a set of purportedly 'recognised' problems and values but also in terms of a set of problems and values that have clearly gripped *other* interesting people around them and before them in the history of political philosophy. Examples of this approach include Wolin's classic *Politics and Vision*,[28] textbooks by the likes of Held,[29] Knowles,[30] and Kymlicka,[31] and edited collec-tions by the likes of White and Moon[32] and Leopold and Stears.[33] They include more esoteric treatments, such as Gunnell's *The Descent of Political Theory* and Vincent's *The Nature of Political Theory*.[34] They include Quinton's equating of our subject with whatever concepts appear central to both past philosophy and contemporary political science[35] and also Blau's identification of something more specific – *analytical* political theory – with both a set of people (Cohen, Dworkin, Nussbaum, Rawls) and a set of commitments that he takes from yet a further pair of individuals trying to define our subject– Miller and Dagger.[36] In each of these cases, then – and this is the point – not only is political philosophy being defined in terms of a set of 'shared' or 'recognised' problems and values, it's also being defined in terms of a set of problems and values clearly attributable to a wider set of authors who collectively count as a 'field', a 'discipline', or, indeed, a historical 'canon'.

Clearly, this seems a sensible way of doing things, so we might just ask here, why *wouldn't* you define political philosophy this way? After all, just as societies operate and innovate within traditions, so do academic disciplines. Peer review, the gold standard of all that we do, is part of this process, and, with each us having but one mind, why not share from the greater 'hive', past and present? Why not, that is, draw on the choices made by many people around and before us – clever people who devoted their lives to this subject, and who have often thought about it much longer than you or I have? Doing so, surely, would lay all our ghosts to rest.

*And yet*, we might feel a little unease here about both who's making the choice and why they're making it. After all, each of these authors has had to *decide* which texts, authors, problems, values, and so on, are definitive for them – just as *I* have had to decide which authors to cite in the preceding paragraphs. And that, unfortunately, gives us two very specific worries. First, a worry about *regression* – where does the relying upon others end? Plato? Socrates? Some lost influence on both of them? Second, a worry about *power* – who is allowed, and who is not allowed, to engage in this defining? Presumably, if we define political philosophy as whatever illustrious individuals have defined it as, we are very likely to be invoking people from just a small set of universities (with particular backgrounds, publishing opportunities, etc.). Presumably, at some point, these people are just defining the subject as they see fit, without relying upon the definitions of others. Presumably, in doing so, they are exercising what Lukes once dubbed the 'second dimension' of power, just insofar as they are setting an agenda for us that influences both the problems we focus on and the way we think about them, to the neglect of things we might never have thought about.[37] Presumably, therefore, when we reproduce or draw on this work, we are simply extending that power.

Yet perhaps we are getting a bit carried away here. After all, we go to doctors for our bodies, mechanics for our cars, and architects for our buildings, in each case recognising something we normally call *expertise*. If, for example, I am lying on a hospital bed, needing urgent medical treatment, am I really going to refuse treatment from the doctor standing before me, trained at Harvard Medical School, just because I worry about the elitism behind her acquired knowledge? If she knows what she's doing then she knows what she's doing. If she's the best in the business then so be it. Why be a fool and ignore such authority? Or consider, if modern economics starts with Adam Smith's *The Wealth of Nations*; if modern biology centres on Darwin's *Origin of Species*, or even Crick and Watson's work on DNA; if modern science and mathematics more generally can't be done without Isaac Newton, then should I jettison all those people just because they are, or were, not only white European males but *British* ones to boot? Whether I like it not, I can't do anything about the fact that, in the long arc of history, many people simply lacked the opportunities they had to do their work.

This is important because, in the history of our species, some parts of the world clearly provided conditions, for some of the time, in which subjects such as political philosophy could be developed while others did not. Ancient Greece had such conditions for a time and then lost them for the next two thousand years. Europe was a relative backwater, in various ways, compared to Islamic or Chinese civilisation in the thousand-year period between the fall of the Roman Empire and the 'discovery' of America, before becoming the place in which modern industrialisation, democracy, and so on, were born. Surely then we don't want to reject modern medicine, technology, and politics just because they came out of *Europe*, and more broadly the *West*, of this period? Surely, in turn, we can't reject the idea of a tradition or canon of political philosophy just because it also came out of those conditions? Shouldn't we then just say something like this: if the best people, when working under the best conditions, came up with *this particular set* of concepts, institutions, problems, values, and so on, then *surely* that's good enough for us.

## 2.5 Despair in the face of incoherence

Clearly there is a great deal to be said for the idea of accepting certain traditions, yet at this point we need to nudge both it and the problem it was trying to solve to one side. This is because, in dealing with all these problems, we've lost sight of what might prove an even bigger challenge. Bearing in mind Nietzsche's remark that only things with no history can be defined,[38] what we've ignored here is the problem that, even if we *were* to accept one of these lists of problems, tasks, concepts – or even thinkers – as definitive of our subject, we still have no idea what *unifies* those things. This matters because, whatever that traditional list of things was, it would still have to hold some common properties that rendered each of its parts appropriately *political, philosophical*, and *fundamental*. After all, we wouldn't want to say that a 'key' concept, such as justice, is a key concept *just* because lots of people said it was. There would, in other words, have to be some explanation of why that concept *counted* as a central one to political philosophy, beyond its praises having been sung by a chorus of philosophers down the years. Otherwise we might be working not just with faulty values or insuperable problems but also with things that are just *irrelevant* – the equivalent of a smuggled-in recipe for chicken vindaloo that, for whatever reason, tickled the fancy of too many smart people down the years. Nowadays most people would laugh if you were to say that politics should be defined and organised in accordance with God's will, with the job of political philosophy then being to interpret the scripture that conveys it. Yet how do we know that this is not precisely what those scholars just canvassed are doing, only with ancient Greek and modern European saints instead of a set of prophets from the Middle East?

This worry tells us something important. It tells us

that we need an account of the key elements of political philosophy that *explains* why these elements *are* part of a single activity – and in a moment I want to provide just that. Before then, however, we need to bring together all of the problems discussed so far, including this last one, so that they are all clearly on display. We can do this by aggregating them as follows. First, bearing in mind the earlier single-concept and single-institution approaches, what we've been trying to avoid is an account that becomes too *narrow* by excluding what we might want to include in our subject. For example, if we make the subject about justice, then what about legitimacy, as many contemporary 'realists' would stress?[39] If we make it about the state, then what about the globe when taken as a whole, as 'cosmopolitans' would urge us?[40] Second, bearing in mind the complications with the multi-problem and interpretation approaches just considered, we've also been trying to avoid an account that is too *broad*. For example, in trying to provide a more 'inclusive' or 'representative' version of our subject, we might produce a disparate list of thinkers, problems, concepts, and so on, with no clear connection between them and with a nagging worry in the air about how arbitrarily they were selected, however long that list becomes. This is a problem illustrated most recently with the rise of ever larger 'handbooks' in both political philosophy and its cognate disciplines. Over time, in order to be more inclusive and comprehensive, the number of topics and chapters goes up and up, yet always without any adequate explanation of what they all have in common, or indeed of why some of them don't belong elsewhere.

## 2.6 Defining with a question

How, then, can we have an account of political philosophy that is both sufficiently inclusive and sufficiently exclusive and which can successfully explain what it has included and excluded? The answer, I think, is a question. That is, I suggest that we adopt as our account of our subject not a simple concept or institution, or indeed a more complex list or tradition of such things, but, rather, what I will call an 'organising question'. This four-part question is as follows: '*How – should – we – live?*' This question 'organises' our subject, or so I will claim, in the sense that it provides it with both a focus and a starting point.

So how exactly does it manage that? It does so, as desired, by being both exclusive and inclusive to just the right degree. This becomes clear when we consider, first of all, how it carves off political philosophy from two further fields that we have not yet discussed but from which we need it to be separate: *moral philosophy*, on the one hand, and *social science* (including political science), on the other. Expanding on this question-as-definition approach, we can now define moral philosophy as being centred on 'How should *I* live?', and social science as centred on 'How *do* we live?' The first subject, we now see, is rendered personal (about *me*) but normative (about what *should* be the case). The second, in turn, becomes collective (again about *us*) but empirical (about what *is* or *has been* the case in the world). So, what we have at this stage, in virtue of these three questions, is a subject that is exclusive from at least two subjects to which it is related, but from which it needs to be separated if we are to have some sense of what does and does not belong within it.

# What?

Now consider inclusiveness. Here the trick is that, by defining political philosophy this way, we manage to include everything we already standardly recognise as being part of the subject – arguments about what the *state* should do, arguments about what *justice* is, and so on – yet without equating it with any one such concern. Compare, for example, our four-part question with other questions we might have used as possible definitions. Unlike 'What sort of government ought we to have?', it avoids the anarchist's response 'Why have any *government* at all?' Unlike 'What is the ideal form of human organisation?', it avoids the communitarian response 'Why just *one* ideal form for everyone?' Unlike 'What does morality require of politics?', it avoids the Hobbesian response 'Why not treat *rationality*, rather than morality, as our guide to normative political enquiry (and perhaps order or happiness, rather than justice, as the object of political design)?'

We also see this inclusiveness when noting the versatility of each of the three constituent parts of our four-word question. The 'How ... live' of 'How should we live?' is open to any form of collective regulation (or deregulation) – state, global government, anarchist commune, and so on. The 'should' could be a 'should' of morality or rationality, depending on your view of such things. The 'we', finally, could be a 'we' of all human beings or of the members of a single faith, community, locality, nation, and so on. Again, then, all the different ways of doing political philosophy we recognise are in there, and none are ruled out right from the start.

This blend of exclusiveness and inclusiveness gives us both focus and flexibility. Focus – because we can be precise about who we are and what we're doing.

Flexibility – because we can accommodate all the different ways of doing and conceiving of our subject currently in fashion. Yet it also gives us something else. It gives us our desired *coherence*, and thus a confidence in what we're doing that we might otherwise lack. We no longer have to worry that the topic we're working on just *happens* to be a topic in our field because someone influential in the past happened to be interested in it. We are no longer basing our list of concepts, values, problems, institutions, and so on, simply on a tradition, however much accumulated wisdom that tradition reflects. And, relatedly, we no longer have to worry that this tradition might be troublingly Western-centric or some such thing. We have not ruled out religious forms of 'should', we have not ruled out the 'we' being some non-Western group of people, and we clearly have not ruled out, from the start, non-liberal versions of 'How … live'.[41] We now have *good reason* for saying that certain things are in and certain things are out, just as we have *no reason* to worry that my work on rights over here has no connection with your work on the virtue required by politicians over there. Now we can say that they're *all* contributions to a single field; that they're *all* political philosophy. Or, put more boldly, but also more clearly: we can now understand all existing work in political theory/philosophy as either an answer or a contribution to an answer to this question: *How should we live?*

## 2.7 A second question and an alternative question

There is, though, a further reason for approving of this question-as-definition, which is that, as soon as it is asked, we are connected, naturally, to yet a further enquiry that sits at the heart of our subject – *Why* should we live that way and not another? Consider here that, if you ask a political philosopher 'How should we live?', the first thing she will probably say is that she cannot tell you how to live every last aspect of your life. She will, though, if you press her, normally offer up something like 'Well, I do think your life ought to be lived in accordance with (or governed by, regulated by, constrained by, etc.) such and such principles' (say, liberal principles). As a result, we could then ask 'Why those principles and not another set?', to which she might reply 'Because these principles correspond to some further set of principles or values' (say, utilitarian principles). And so it would go on – maybe not forever: at some point she might just say 'These are your values' or 'Rationality requires these commitments of you' – but, nonetheless, there will be a chain of 'whys' leading up to the final 'how', with those 'whys' making up most of the argument we would hear, or indeed see if you were following it in a book or article. Nozick's famous *Anarchy, State, and Utopia*, for example, answers the question 'How should we live?' by saying, early on, that we should live in fairly minimalist 'night-watchman' states of the kind that classical libertarians and modern neoliberals dream of. Most of the book, naturally, is devoted to *why* we should do so.

This pay-off, according to which an 'organising' question both leads us to and explains the importance of subordinate questions, is something we can also see in other fields. Consider, for example, the possibility of defining medical research in terms of two organising questions: (1) How can we prolong life? (2) How can we reduce pain? With these two general questions in mind, you can quickly see how one's research might branch out into: How do kidneys work as they age? What are stem cells? How do mice genetically differ from humans? And so on. Those first two questions, in other words, *organise* medical research just insofar as they *make sense* of it, with the latter questions naturally subordinated to them. They get *their* meaning and purpose just insofar as they are answers or contributions to those first two questions. Similarly, in political philosophy, if we know that we are trying to find an answer, or at least part of the answer, to the question 'How should we live?', then we know why we care about questions such as: What are human rights?, or Do I owe more to my compatriots than to foreigners born 10,000 miles away?, or Should goods be distributed according to how hard we work or how much we need?, or Should the wisest people be in charge or the ones who represent us best? And so on and so forth.

We might, however, agree at this stage that our subject *could* be defined or organised with a question yet disagree that the *particular* one I have suggested is the best option. And, indeed, we might even think that just a small change to my suggested question would help things. This change would give us the following alternative question, 'How should we live *together*?', though we might also go for something like 'How should we regulate our *collective* existence?' Both of these questions, clearly, are plausible definitions, and perhaps even ones that others might have offered if asked. Barry, for example, once wrote that 'justice as impartiality' is an answer to the problem of 'how to live together',[42] while Gibbard, slightly more confusingly from our point of view, writes that moral thinking in general is 'thinking how to live with each other',[43] with 'ethical theory' defined in a later passage as 'planning how to live with each other'.[44] Miller and Dagger, rather less confusingly, talk at one point of 'how people should live in societies and order their common affairs'.[45]

How then could we choose between these similar yet alternative questions? After all, doesn't politics and political philosophy only begin once the 'we' in my question starts to work 'together' as a 'society'? Remember, though, what this question needs to achieve. Although it's fine if it leads us to ever narrower and subordinate questions – recall the philosopher from a moment ago who admitted they couldn't tell us how to live every aspect of our lives – it's also crucial that it doesn't close off important options from the start, which is precisely what happens once we add in these clauses of 'together' or 'community'. This is because we cannot assume, from the off, that we will always want to live together, even if we need to do so for now. Many of us, after all, agree with Sartre's remark that 'hell is other people', even if we tend to vary the phrase from day to day, so that it specifies, say, colleagues, neighbours, and so on. As a parent, for example, I tend to think that hell is other people's children. Maybe the real dream for all or at least some of us, therefore, once it's available, is to be hooked into a new 'Matrix', digitally engaging with others who match us or even fictional others who appreciate us as much as we appreciate ourselves. Isn't that, after all, the direction in which social media and virtual reality are already heading?

Yet even without such utopian (or dystopian) dreams, it is enough here to look at what anarchists and some

libertarians have long wanted: as loose and as volun-
tary an association as possible, with no collective rules
or organisations constraining this choice of 'how we
live'. Of course, you might disagree with that and say
that anarchists are fools who fight the state only to let
companies, bullies, and bandits run things, but that is
not the point. The point is that, as soon as you're doing
that, you are *doing* political philosophy, and effectively
saying that anarchists have a *bad* answer to our organising question – How should we live? And, again, that's
fine, just so long as we don't rule out anarchism from
the start. Naturally, not everyone can win the race, but
everyone deserves a place at the starting line – or at
least everyone does who plans on running the race as
opposed to doing something else altogether, such as
moral philosophy, political science, or cookery.

### 2.8 What form do the answers take? Principles or manifestos? Blueprints or red lines?

Now just one last puzzle. Miller and Dagger write at
one point, in their aforementioned discussion of 'analytical' political theory, that it seeks to 'establish political
principles that can govern the constitution of states and
the making of public policy'.[46] This raises an interesting
challenge, hovering at the edges of the question of 'What
is political philosophy?', though in danger of straying
into 'How do we do it?' – the challenge of figuring
out exactly what it is we are *producing* when providing answers to our organising question. Are we, for
example, providing general and abstract principles or
detailed political-party manifestos? Are we offering up
a set of instructions that tells people exactly what to do,

or simply providing a set of rules that tells them what not to do? So, *detail* or *generalities*, how we *should* live or maybe just how we *should not* live?

My answer to this puzzle is that, yes, we are working, primarily, in *principles* rather than *precise* policies, but also that it cannot be decided from the outset whether we're working on a set of 'dos' or 'don'ts'. That second issue is one for political philosophy proper – not my discussion of its nature here. It is something we find out only once we start arguing, and we ought not to include or exclude it from the start. Returning to the first issue, though, we should certainly be worrying about principles, such as 'maximise individual liberty to the extent that it is compatible with an equal liberty for all', or 'all beneficiaries of a system of co-operation should pay a fair share of whatever is required to maintain it', or 'a state should only interfere with the lives of an individual or group in order to prevent that individual or group from harming others.' Or, put differently, we should be arguing about which of these principles, and which combination of these principles, functions as the best possible answer to the question 'How should we live?'

Why, though, this insistence on principles? Well, the logic is simple. First, consider here that principles are simply general rules fit for expression through actions or institutions. A politician, for example, can *act* on the basis of a principle or set of principles, just as an electoral system could *instantiate* such things. Second, consider that, if political philosophers devoted themselves to, say, telling people how to vote in an upcoming UK general election, then what they're doing is of limited use. Its value has evaporated as soon as the election is over. Third, consider that, even if they did offer such advice, it would logically have to be based on more general reasoning – remember, the 'whys' always follow the 'hows'. If I told you, for example, to vote for the British Labour Party, you would naturally ask why. I might then say that it's because Labour offer the right balance of liberty and equality. You would then ask why that is the right balance. I would then give you some reasons, perhaps tapping into values you already recognise, or perhaps showing you that other ways of thinking about liberty and equality just don't work – but, either way, notice that, as soon as I'm doing that, I'm now doing something quite important.

That is, once I'm saying that you should think *this* way about equality and liberty, I am in effect telling you that this is how you should *always* think about equality and liberty. I can't tell you that this is just how you should think about it today *without* implying that it should also be seen this way tomorrow. I might tell you, of course, that you should only vote Labour *if* certain conditions pertain, but, again, if I do that, then I'm saying that, *whenever* such conditions pertain, you should *always* vote Labour. In this way, principles are inseparable from policies, whatever campaign strategists might believe. One simply cannot argue for any given policy without drawing on principles which, if they ever apply to a given situation, must always apply to all equivalent situations, with yet some further argument sitting right around the corner regarding how those situations differ and what to do when that happens. Of course, front-line politicians often manage perfectly well without digging too deep into those principles, but even for them it can often be fatal not really to know what lies behind their slogans. In the 2017 UK general election, for example, Theresa May quickly got into trouble for simply repeating, in every interview, her mantra of 'strong and stable government' (versus a 'coalition of chaos') without being able to provide a proper account of its underlying logic. This earned her the nickname 'Maybot', as well as distracting from what might well have been similar problems for Labour's slogan of 'for the many, not the few'.

Saying, however, that we are *always* interested in principles does *not* mean that we don't also want to see how those principles apply in particular situations, such as this or that election, or war, or climate-change treaty. It's just that the principles are the key – and in much the same way as when we noted earlier the distinction between a fundamental organising question and the subordinate questions to which it leads. Remember here, after all, that when thinking about principles that answer our question – *How should we live?* – we might only be working on one *small* part of that question. We might ask, for example: What is power, or what kinds of power are there? What kinds of liberty and equality are there, and what are their strengths and weaknesses? What is justice, and how might it tell us how to rank or trade off those liberties and equalities? What is legitimacy, and how might it tell us who gets to decide on this or that account of justice? What is democracy, and how might thinking about its forms and dimensions help us work out the requirements of legitimacy? What is a nation, and does one need one in order to have the kind of *demos* required of democracy? How should we think about gender and culture in order to ensure that that *demos* acts and is represented accordingly? And so on and so forth. All of these questions need examining so that we have the materials out of which principles can be built. All of these questions need examining so that we can consider various answers to our earlier 'working definition' of political philosophy, namely, 'What *should* politics be like?' All of them need examining, more precisely, so that we can consider various answers to our new, four-part, and organising question for our subject, namely, *'How – should – we – live?'*

# 3
# How?

## 3.1 Introduction

This chapter explains how to do political philosophy by explaining its three constitutive tasks: *analysis, critique,* and *ordering.* These are the tasks we undergo when trying to provide either an answer, or a contribution to an answer, to our subject's organising question: How should we live? Roughly speaking, each of them works as follows. First, we *analyse* when setting out the ideas we need to think about when organising our political existence – concepts of power and exploitation, principles of justice and legitimacy, and so on. Second, we *critique* when providing warnings about those ideas – the dangerous implications of Isaiah Berlin's 'positive freedom', the inconsistency in John Stuart Mill's 'harm principle', the dubious ideological or evolutionary roots to our attachments to capitalism, nationhood, and so on. Third, we *order* when providing arguments about how to rank and prioritise the ideas we have analysed and critiqued – arguments that give us comprehensive cases for pursuing, say, a particular concept of liberty, a particular principle of justice, a particular version of democracy, or a particular way of organising international politics.

These three tasks, we should note from the start, are complementary, not competitive, and not just due to mutual compatibility but also because the first supports the second, which in turn supports the third. Clearly, we need to know the dimensions of our ideas before assessing their dangers, and we need to know both before turning them into a co-ordinated set of ideals we need to adopt – just as an architect needs to know the working materials she has available, together with their strengths and weaknesses, before planning the building she is about to construct, or indeed inhabit. As a result, I do not call these three tasks 'alternative methods' or 'rival approaches', as they might be labelled in some places.[1] That would be a mistake here. What they are is co-operative contributions to a shared endeavour, not rival versions of a subject that could not even contain rivals, logically speaking, were it not for the fact that it is defined by a single purpose, as given by our single, organising question.

These three tasks, when seen in action, also serve to reinforce the centrality of that organising question. We might, for example, look at various well-known analyses of power, freedom, or equality.[2] We might look at famous egalitarian critiques of libertarianism or libertarian critiques of egalitarianism.[3] Or we might look, with ordering in mind, at the latest arguments for this or that view of legitimacy, each of which not only helps us answer our organising question but might be as much of an answer as we can *ever* offer, depending on how much scope for real-world variation our arguments tell us is appropriate.[4] In each of these cases – and this is the point – we are clearly producing something which either answers or helps to answer our subject's organising question. And, note, the term 'we' is important here, given that it might turn out that no scholar *alone* could ever provide such an answer. Together though, as political philosophers, this is our collective mission: to undertake one or more of these three tasks in order to tell us how politics *should* work, assuming we should have any politics at all; to tell us, in as much detail as possible, *how we should live*.

Now one last point before exploring these three activities. Consider here, early on, and before we lose our way, that the 'how' of this chapter could easily slip into the 'what' of the previous chapter or even the 'why' of the next. We might, for example, *define* political philosophy in terms of one or more of these tasks, in which case we would be doing something similar to the 'problem-based' definitions discussed in chapter 2, as drawn from Cohen, Waldron, and Rawls. Similarly, we might answer the question of 'Why do political philosophy?' just by saying, Well, it addresses intrinsically *interesting* concepts, such as power and justice, and answers an intrinsically interesting organising question, in which case there is nothing more to say. Both slips, I think, are tempting, but also mistaken. As explained in the previous chapter, it would be a mistake to define our subject in terms of a set of tasks or methods unless we could say *what it was that those methods had in common* or how they counted as components of a *single* subject. We can only do that when one has in mind the more fundamental challenge they are helping to address. Similarly, it would be a mistake to limit the *purpose* of our subject with the goals of the tasks set out in this chapter. Although it is indeed interesting to analyse power, criticise equality, or provide a compelling answer to the wider question 'How should we live?', that still wouldn't *fully* explain *why*, precisely, one would want to write up such an answer in an esoteric article or book which, in all likelihood, only a handful of people will ever read. Intrinsic interest explains part of the 'point' of political philosophy, but not the whole point. If, as I say in the next chapter, a key part of the point of political philosophy is to change the world, then we need to know how our academic work helps us to do that.

## 3.2 Analysis

Consider here that, if you want to find out how politics *should* work, then what you'll need, first of all, are *ideas*. You'll need, that is, to know the nuts and bolts you're working with. Or, more precisely, you'll need to know two things: (1) the *variables* to control and distribute, such as freedom, power, or justice; and (2) the *problems* to avoid, such as discrimination, exploitation, or domination. Exploring these two things is the business of our first task, *analysis*.

How, though, do we do this? We do it by focusing on our *language* and *feelings*[5] in order to isolate the concepts they convey – with *concepts* here meaning the particular variable-ideas and problem-ideas we are interested in. For example, I might be curious about the term 'equality', perhaps expecting it to be an ideal around which I would like to organise my politics. To begin with, I think about all the different ways I use that term – the situations to which it pertains, the goods it measures, and so on. Then, after a while, I realise that I am working with at least two concepts rather than one. Although there seems to be a general concept of equality, in terms of 'sameness' or 'parity', it turns out that there are at least two more specific concepts – equality of *condition* and equality of *opportunity*. We have equality of condition, I realise, when two or more individuals or groups have the same amount of something: when we have the same amount of money, for instance, or when we are equally tall, attractive, or strong. We have equality of opportunity, I now see, when we have the same options – schools, jobs, partners, and so on.[6] So, just as one could start off with the general concept of 'dog' before identifying the more specific concepts of 'poodle' and 'labrador' (or indeed 'labradoodle'), here we started off with the general 'species' of equality before picking out just two of its key political breeds, 'condition' and 'opportunity'.

This dividing and labelling continues until we've made things as specific as they need to be for us to figure out our political ambitions. For example, when thinking about equality of opportunity, I might further distinguish between 'formal' and 'substantive' equality of opportunity. We have the latter, I discover, when 'those with similar abilities and skills have similar life chances';[7] we have the former simply when there is no discrimination against me when I apply for, say, a job or an educational opportunity. Formal equality of opportunity, I notice, focuses on things such as racism or religious intolerance, while substantive equality takes account of things such as poverty and private education, but also potentially our friendship groups, given the networking connections they afford, or even bed-time stories, given that, if some parents read stories to their kids and others do not, that can create an inequality as regards the relative capabilities, and then life chances, of the two sets of children.

At all times here, then, what we're doing with this kind of analysis is clarifying the ideas with which we're working by breaking them apart into their key elements and then bringing those elements into high definition. This is the immediate aim of our activity, though, when doing so, it's worth bearing in mind that sometimes by-products of this process turn out to be more important than the ideas we (thought we) started off with. For example, when analysing equality, as considered so far, I might eventually come to realise that the thing I *really* cared about when using this term was actually *not equality at all*. Perhaps, when I used this term in connection with society's worst-off, what I was *really* aiming for was the alleviation of poverty. Perhaps, therefore, what I really care about, deep down, is simply that everyone has what they *need*, or *enough*, and not that everyone has the *same* of everything. I am bothered by the child living in destitution, for example, but not by the pay gap between a stockbroker and her line manager. In this case, my key concept would no longer be equality but, rather, *priority* or *sufficiency*, because I now realise I want to *prioritise* society's worst-off – the poor, the needy, the deprived – and ensure that what they have is *sufficient* for their needs, regardless of, say, the income gap between the median and top earners.[8] It turns out that it's their *needs*, ultimately, that drive me, not the degree of inequality between them and others, and certainly not the degree of inequality between the rich and the very rich.

Now, all this talk of what I 'care about' or what 'drives me' takes us back to something I said a moment ago – about how one works with feelings as well as language when undertaking conceptual analysis. This is important given that, when figuring out our key concepts, we are interested not just in the different ways in which we use a term but also in our evaluative responses to the different situations and actions to which they pertain. My getting *angrier* about poverty than about inequality, for example, helped me realise that something like 'sufficiency' could be the centrepiece of my politics. Or, if I thought there's something wrong with racial discrimination but not with kids' bed-time stories, then that can help me to see the distinction between substantive and formal equality of opportunity.

Consider also that we can even *start* with these feelings, just as one might in *psycho*analysis. We might, for example, start with our *outrage* at something, or a practice we just *know* to be bad, even if we can't articulate as yet just what it is that is bad about it. We might say for instance, that we know that slavery is wrong, yet wonder precisely *why* it is wrong. Thinking about it, and comparing the case of the slave to the case of, say, a sadomasochist or an indentured labourer, we might come to believe that this is because it involves the lack of a particular kind of *freedom* that we end up calling *autonomy* – the ideal of a self-directed life. In this case, we would have arrived at *that* particular concept by starting with a situation that lacked it. And, indeed, we might even go on to say that this concept also makes sense of our disdain for yet further situations, such as

49

feudalism, or even just a minority democratic franchise – all situations in which, to various degrees, people have their lives run by others over whom they have no say. So, just as we work with our language in order to bring our key ideas to light, we do the same thing, and often at the same time, with our feelings.

Notice also here that in these recent examples we've been talking about *problems* as well as *variables*, as indicated at the start of this section. We are interested, that is, not just in the concepts out of which we want to build our political order – equality, autonomy, power, and so on – but also in the challenges we want that order to address – inequality, domination, and so forth. This is as expected, though it raises an interesting question, namely, do all our problems only *count* as such because they violate our value-variables? For example, how could one explain discrimination without being able to say that it's a failure of equality or justice? How could one explain domination or exploitation without saying that each of them is a failure of liberty? Of course, we might only discover those values by starting with these problems,[9] but that wouldn't change the relationship unless it turned out that we could only describe our variables in terms of the problems they are meant to solve. In that case, problems, rather than the variables they reveal, would be our fundamental unit of analysis.

Clearly, this is an interesting puzzle, as well as one that reminds us of our challenge in the previous chapter with concepts versus institutions. Yet it's also a sideshow, given that there's nothing to stop us here from analysing *both* problems and variables, however reciprocal those two jobs become. There is, however, a more important issue that this puzzle touches upon, namely, are the concepts we are analysing things that we are *discovering* or things we are *inventing*?

This is an argument we can again make in either direction. On the one hand, if what we are doing is isolating and dividing the terms we *already use* and picking apart the feelings we *already have*, then it seems as though discovery is the more appropriate term. We are, after all, simply bringing into focus concepts that we were already using, though we didn't know we were doing so. We are finding the DNA in the nucleus or the ore in the rock – we are not putting it there ourselves. *And yet*, on the other hand, invention might be more apt, given that we often seem to come up with *new* ideas. Key contemporary terms of jargon in political philosophy, such as 'prioritarian' or 'substantive equality of opportunity', simply did not exist before somebody proposed them.

Perhaps, then, a better term than either of these two would be *innovation*. We innovate when discovering new concepts, just by splitting apart the ones we already use, but also when inventing new ones, because even when they are very novel indeed they are still developed out of pre-existing materials. We are, therefore, to borrow a metaphor I used earlier, something like dog-breeders, or perhaps genetic engineers. Rather than simply observing what is already 'out there' in the world, we play around with it, combining different things, and seeing what we end up with. Think here, for example, of Plato's famous vision of an ideal republic. Clearly, this is a complicated, composite, and original concept made up of still smaller complicated, composite, and original concepts – including his unique notion of justice – yet, in its most basic ingredients, it is still composed of elemental concepts with which all of us already think. And, note, this historical parallel is especially appropriate if we recall that philosophy *in general* was once described as 'footnotes to Plato',[10] a claim which, in this context, means not that he was *not* an innovator – for he was – but simply that he was *more* innovative than anyone either before or after him in the history of our field. He was, in other words, writing 'footnotes' himself – to his own feelings, to the language of his times, to his own interlocutors, and of course to whatever earlier thinkers and texts he could access, even when we have lost sight of them. So, as with the builders of the Acropolis, a sight Plato could gaze up at every day, it is not that they were inventing new 'stones', it is just that what was being done with them was more original, and grander, than anything that had gone before.

Historical examples like these also have a further benefit here, which is that they help to make sense of a further resource upon which political philosophers often draw when conducting analysis: the study of the *history* of our subject. Quentin Skinner, for example, contributed to our understanding of freedom when he excavated a 'neo-Roman' concept of liberty before comparing it with Thomas Hobbes's thoughts on the same subject.[11] Philip Pettit, among others, labelled that concept 'republican' liberty before organising a wider political vision around it.[12] In both cases, we see again that mixture of discovery and invention that is best described as innovation. There is, however, something distinctive here about this historical route in terms of how we map out our concepts – a third resource to draw upon, beyond our current language and feelings. Consider here, for example, the popular project of analysing freedom, as shared by Skinner and Pettit. Naturally, your own language and feelings will be your first port of call, as well as the final arbiter in your analysis, given that a set of political concepts with no purchase whatsoever in those things will have little place in your affections, and by extension your politics. Then, as a second resource, you have the best pieces of contemporary scholarship as you look to make sense of such language and feelings. But then, as a final option, you have a third resource in history. We might, for example, find it helpful to turn to Rousseau's distinction between natural, civil, and moral liberty or Constant's distinction between the liberties of the 'ancients' and the 'moderns', especially when combined with the kind of work produced by Skinner and Pettit.[13]

How though, exactly, does all this analysis help us to figure out how politics *should* be organised? It does so, once again, by laying the groundwork for our two further tasks – critique and ordering. As explained, this is a natural relationship, though there is, as it happens, a historical trend that illustrates it well. Consider here that, in the anglophone world following the Second World War, conceptual analysis, as it is often called, was all the rage. Indeed, it often seemed like the *definitive* activity of what then seemed to count as *all* philosophy – *analytic* philosophy – while its commitment to conceptual clarity and transparency remains with us today in our subject's common self-description as *analytical* political philosophy.[14] Highlights of this era include Brian Barry's *Political Argument*,[15] David Lyons's *Forms and Limits of Utilitarianism*,[16] Bernard Williams's 'The idea of equality',[17] and also 'meta-conceptual' pieces such as Gallie's 'Essentially contested concepts'.[18] Yet the most discussed piece, by some way, is Isaiah Berlin's 'Two concepts of liberty'.[19] This is a work we touched on just a moment ago when discussing Skinner and Pettit, and it's telling that, even for them, with historical scholarship so important, it was really Berlin's essay that functioned as the key intellectual starting point.[20] Their project, in effect, has been one of saying that there are really *three* concepts of liberty, whereas Berlin's earlier achievement was to make people think that there might be *two* concepts rather than one, with each reflecting what he called a particular 'attitude to the ends of life'.[21] In other words, they developed *his* work at least as much as they developed the work of those older historical figures, whom they claimed Berlin's analysis had neglected.

Yet how does any of this illustrate the 'natural' relationship I have in mind between analysis, critique, and ordering? The key point is that this 'development' of Berlin's work is typical of what came next in the subject, as the analyses of the 1950s and 1960s started to become building blocks for the far grander projects of the subsequent decades. When John Rawls published *A Theory of Justice*[22] in 1971, for example, he drew on, *inter alia*, Barry,[23] Lyons,[24] Williams,[25] and Berlin,[26] as well as the wider web of concepts and arguments to which they contributed, even though his ultimate ambition differed starkly from any of theirs. His project was to provide an argument for a specific *ordering* of principles to which he gave the name *Justice as Fairness* – an achievement often described as a 'watershed', 'break' or 'rebirth' moment in the history of our field, which is true, as far as it goes. Certainly, he was returning our subject to an earlier and grander focus on producing arguments for particular and *ordered* sets of principles. Yet it's also true that his work drew, as it must, on the

earlier *analyses* of his contemporaries and predecessors
– as well as on their *critiques*, to which we turn in a
moment. Clearly he was a key 'innovator', in our earlier
language, and clearly his work marks a major 'watershed', yet the term 'break' is misleading. He built, as all
great thinkers do, on the work of his predecessors.

It might help then, at this point, to describe the
relationship like this: in analysing our problems and variables, we lay the *groundwork* for critique and ordering.
For critique, because only when we isolate things into
their smallest parts, and bring them fully into focus, can
we begin to criticise them. For ordering, because only
when we have done both of these things can we begin to
argue about which variables and problems to prioritise.
For example, in order to criticise 'substantive' equality
of opportunity on the grounds that it might mean inter-
fering with children's bed-time stories, we need first to
have separated it from 'formal' equality of opportunity,
with both already having been carved off from 'equality
of condition'. And, in turn, when it comes to ordering,
for me to argue about whether I should prioritise, say,
formal equality of opportunity or autonomy – another
ideal discussed earlier – I need first to see the critiques to
which both can be subjected.

But let's not get ahead of ourselves here. In order to
perform either *critique* or *ordering* in a proper manner,
we still need to look carefully at the second key concept
we've been using in this section – this idea of 'variables'.
This means noticing, in particular, that often the variables we want to pursue are not *values*, such as liberty, or
even *resources*, such as power, but rather *principles*, the
very purpose of which is to tell us just how such values
and resources ought to be distributed. As explained in

the previous chapter, it is principles rather than party manifestos that ultimately concern us when pursuing an answer to our 'organising question'. Or, put differently, it is a clear principle, or set of principles, that we want to emerge out of the process of ordering that we come to later on. As explained in chapter 2, these principles, whether of justice or legitimacy, take the form of general rules capable of guiding either individual behaviour or institutional design. They are things that we can abide by or which our institutions can reflect, and as such they give us the guidance we need when figuring out how to organise our political system – assuming, that is, that we don't end up affirming anarchist principles, and thus wanting no system at all.

Now, analysis is crucial here because the analysed differences *between* principles can be all the difference in the world. Consider, for example, morality's so-called golden rule – treat others as you would yourself like to be treated. This principle derives its 'golden' status both from the possibility that it might explain all our further and more particular normative judgements and from the fact that versions of it can be found in most moral traditions – Christian, Islamic, Judaic, Confucian, Enlightenment, and so on. Yet what's really fascinating about it is that one can split it, conceptually speaking, into at least two variants, both of which are found in each tradition: (1) 'Do to others that which you would have done to yourself'[27] and (2) 'Do *not* do to others that which you would not have done to yourself.'[28] Linguistically, of course, the difference here is small, but in politics, and indeed in life more generally, it is vast. It is the difference, after all, between *helping* and simply *not hindering*; between egalitarianism and libertarianism; and, for many people, though they might not realise it, between left-wing and right-wing affiliations. This is why analysis is so important: it gives us a precise focus on important distinctions that would otherwise escape us. It enables us to see just what the key variants are of some crucial ideas and then, in turn, just where those variants begin to lead. In this case, it meant noticing that people often split on this very fundamental distinction, whether they realise it or not, and identifying something that helps to explain so many of their other commitments. And it means something else. It means isolating things that one can either *critique* or argue in favour of as part of an overall *ordering*.

How far though, exactly, can one go with this kind of analysis? This is an important question, bearing in mind that some scholars think there are, in truth, *no* further tasks beyond analysis, or at least beyond analysis with just a little bit of critique – to which we turn in a moment. This would be true, for example, if one believed in a more general idea to which Isaiah Berlin subscribed but which has been developed in more sophisticated forms since – the idea of 'value-pluralism'.[29] In essence, that idea boils down to two claims. First, there are many ideal ways of living individual lives, and also organising politics, all of which are *incommensurable*, meaning that there is no common measure by which they can all be compared. Second, you can't have them all *at once*. Now, you might reasonably believe in both these claims, and, if so, it might follow that the job of a political philosopher is simply to analyse our concepts, point out their incompatibilities and potential trade-offs, and *then* leave it to individuals and societies to figure out such things for themselves. Of course, that would still be a very useful task – at least if one thinks that having *more* options, and *clearer* ones, is better than fewer and blurred ones – yet it is still a more modest project than most political philosophers have followed in recent decades, just as it is a more modest project than the one described by this book. Our mission, remember, is either to answer or to contribute to an answer to our subject's organising question: *How should we live?*

In summary, then, we can say at this stage that we perform analysis when mapping out either (1) problems we want to avoid, such as discrimination or exploitation, or (2) variables we want to control – resources such as power, values such as freedom, and also principles of justice, legitimacy, and so on. As examples, splitting equality into two separate concepts is part of this task; retrieving an old and forgotten ideal of liberty is part of this task; isolating the value we think lacking in conditions of slavery is part of this task; distinguishing two different versions of morality's 'golden rule' is part of this task; and so on and so forth. In all such cases we learn of new variables and new problems and develop ever more fine-grained lists of items in need of consideration. In all of them, we gather up the material we need for *critique*, which in turn gives us just the materials we want for our arguments about how a particular set of variables should be *ordered*.

## 3.3 Critique

We move now from analysis to critique, while acknowledging that we were already spilling over into it in the last section. For example, when noting that bed-time stories might have to be abolished in the pursuit of substantive equality of opportunity, we were really floating an *objection* to that ideal – given the intrusiveness of such a restriction – and thus in effect mounting a *critique* – a warning that says 'tread carefully' here. Similarly, when Skinner and Pettit argued that there were in fact three concepts of liberty rather than Berlin's two, they did so in part by pointing out the drawbacks of Berlin's notion of 'negative liberty' – explaining how it lacked something that their third concept – 'neo-Roman' or 'republican' liberty – did not. Such spillover is unsurprising, given that a good deal of the 'conceptual analysis' of the 1950s and 1960s involved, at least in part, what we might call 'critical analysis' – a hybrid practice that involves splitting apart the concepts in question while also casting a bad light on at least some of what was laid out. This is a tradition that continues today, though it does so without affecting the key *analytical* point that analysis and critique remain distinct, if combinable, tasks. One can, after all, do analytical work perfectly well without getting into critical territory, or at least the kind of territory I have in mind when using the term 'critique', given that we can criticise a fellow author's analysis without offering political objections to the concepts in question. That qualification, however, and the questions it raises about the nature of 'objections', only hastens the necessity to do what needs to be done in this section, namely, to clarify exactly what critique involves. So, with that in mind, the key claim here is this: critique can be boiled down to just three key varieties – (1) 'dangerous implications', (2) 'inconsistency', and (3) 'suspicious roots'. Each of these is a weapon the political philosopher needs in their arsenal. In what follows, I discuss each of them in turn.

# How?

We start with 'dangerous implications'. Like all forms of critique, it follows on from the kind of conceptual analysis discussed above but then does something quite specific: pointing out the dangers inherent in pursuing or believing in the concepts set out – a problem one might address, a value one might pursue, or a principle one might adopt. Consider then, once more, this central debate to which we keep returning: the debate that started with Berlin's argument that there are in fact two distinct concepts of liberty, each of which, he thought, reflects divergent 'attitudes to the ends of life'.[30] What matters now is that this argument doesn't stop with those claims, because he also went on to argue that, as soon as one pursues 'positive liberty' as an ideal – the idea of being free to do or become things – one is unavoidably committed to some or other idea of 'self-realisation' or 'emancipation' – the notion that each of us has some inner 'potential' which needs to be realised, whether we recognise it yet or not. And indeed, we might think, what is so bad about that?

Yet Berlin saw danger here. He said that, when one is committed to the advancement of positive liberty in others, one all too readily believes at least three things: (1) that there is some ideal way of living that suits all individuals – whether that be a communist bureaucracy, a libertarian free-for-all, a monastic idyll, and so on; (2) that this way would be ideal even for people who didn't recognise this right now in their life goals; and (3) that, when one has worked out this ideal, pretty much any sacrifice would be permissible in the short term in order to get to the kind of utopia we would have once people are living in just that way. According to Berlin, you can see this line of thought in a range of different settings – from the French and Russian revolutions to Nazi Germany – and in all cases see the same vice: this iron belief that, if you're helping people to realise their true, inner potential, as citizens, communists, Aryans, or whatever, then no amount of short-term suffering is too much. Right now, we might say, people are duped by the right-wing press, or lefty social media, or just their boring old parents. Once we drag them into the new political order, they'll soon realise we were right to do so.

Now, keep this argument in mind for a moment while also considering a second and related case. This is the case of Thomas Hobbes, whom again we touched on earlier, and who again, like Berlin, was worried about the dangers of utopianism. He wrote, against much of the intellectual current of his time, that nothing had been more 'deerly bought' in seventeenth-century England than the learning of the Greeks and Romans[31] – filling his country's parliamentarians with dreams of republics and so on. This is because the reality of life without strong and singular leadership, he claimed, is very different from what they imagine. Without it, whoever tries to lead that society will be threatened by others who want to take over, and he or she will have to clamp down viciously in order to stop them. Civil war will emerge from that dynamic, just as it did in republican Rome, and just as was happening in parliamentary England – and nothing, Hobbes thought, was worse than civil war. Once such a war begins, and once there is no guarantee of safety from a common power, then all hell breaks loose. Promises become meaningless without anyone to enforce them, as 'Covenants, without the Sword, are but Words.'[32] Some strike early to avoid being struck later. Others steal in fear of being robbed themselves. There is no building, no 'arts', 'letters', or 'society', and no 'industry', 'because the fruit thereof is uncertain.'[33] And so it continues, from seventeenth-century England to contemporary Syria or Libya: a downward spiral of death and destruction, the ending of which can come only at the hands of – what else? – a strong and singular leader.

As with Berlin's story, in which Nazis relate to Jacobins, Hobbes's anti-utopian argument has many echoes down the years. We see it, for example, in Burke's *Reflections on the Revolution in France* and his prophetic claim that, 'in the groves of their academy, at the end of every vista, you see nothing but the gallows.'[34] We see it in the work of contemporary 'realists' in political philosophy, for whom the targets are not republicans in pursuit of 'mixed government' but Rawlsians in pursuit of justice.[35] And we see it, going back to where we started, in Berlin. Of course, he is no absolutist like Hobbes, yet he shares their wider anti-utopian idea that certain ideals can be as *dangerous* as they are *inspiring*. All that matters here, then, is the common ground shared by these arguments, and in particular the following idea: that objections to a particular position, based on that position's dangerous implications, can weaken our attachment to it without themselves relying on any *alternative* (though of course these authors do have alternatives in mind).

In other words, this kind of critique has real force for us even without the provision of some alternative utopia. That is the key point, as well as the point that marks out the essential form of our first kind of critique. Yet it is not the only point of interest here. Before we get into our two further forms of critique, it is also worth noting that, just as one can turn *analysis* into something like political philosophy's *definitive* activity if one believes in 'value-pluralism' – for, remember, if all good things are incommensurable, there's nothing more to be done besides setting out options and conflicts – one could also think that this kind of critique marks the limits of what we can do, provided that one accepts a certain kind of political 'realism' (and perhaps also value-pluralism alongside it). That is, we might say that the *only* real job for political philosophers is to point out *dangers*, without giving us ideal *orderings* to which we should aspire. Or, to borrow from Hampshire, another realist, we might want to make our aim not the pursuit of a *summum bonum* (greatest good) but simply the avoidance of a *summum malum* (greatest evil).[36] Or, even more precisely, and also more comprehensively, we might put it like this: perhaps the role of political philosophers in our world should simply be to set our *variables* and *problems*, via analysis, before *warning* us about some of them, and then *stopping*. After all, we can be rather dangerous if let loose, as noted by Hobbes and Burke, as illustrated by various Jacobins and communists, and as discussed later on in chapter 4.

Again, though, such restrictions are not part of the plan here, which is why, instead of dwelling on them, we turn now to our second form of critique – 'inconsistency'. This form works by identifying a set of commitments within a given position, and usually within a single author's work, and then showing their incompatibility. Consider, for example, Charles Taylor's argument against Berlin's position in 'Two concepts of liberty', the thrust of which is that the so-called horror of having to make judgements regarding other people's lives, when pursuing positive liberty, is felt *equally* when pursuing negative liberty.[37] This is because, as soon as you try to achieve this 'freedom from constraints', you realise that there are going to be constraints *whatever* you do.

To illustrate this argument, consider here that, while property law restricts my movements, its absence restricts my gardening or smallholding efforts, once people just wander in and out of the land I cultivate. Similarly, traffic lights restrict my driving, yet so does the congestion a lack of them generates. Noise controls restrict the way I play my music, yet noisy neighbours stop me from getting to sleep. So what are we to do? Clearly, as individuals and societies, we have to decide *which* negative liberties, *plural*, matter *more* than others in order to know what to prioritise, and indeed in order to know what would count as 'more' or 'better' negative liberty. And how do we do that? Well, in order to figure out the more *important* liberties we need to know which ones *really matter* to people, which is tricky given how unsure they are themselves on that question, and also given how much they tend to disagree with each other. As a result, what we then have to do is try and work out what their *real interests* are, which means in effect trying to figure out what's *good* for them. And then – oh dear, look where we've arrived: back with making judgements about people's interests, or, as Taylor and others often call it, their 'conception of the good'.[38]

This argument, if correct, has serious consequences, including the point that, once we come to see the supposed *neutrality* of negative liberty as an illusion, we soon come to see the failure of that ideal to prop up the popular political idea of 'neutral' and 'free' markets. This is because, as we now see, rolling back the state and advancing private property doesn't really give people *more* negative liberty in any simple sense, with it then just being up to them what they do with it. It simply restricts them in some ways but not others, just as it works well for some people but not others. As a result, what we are doing here with this argument, when identifying the inconsistency in Berlin's position, is really quite important. We are revealing it as being not just less convincing than we might have thought but also less useful as a means of propping up wider political positions.

Now, though, we need to gather up a second example of this form of critique, bearing in mind, once again, that key point from earlier – that we're advancing these arguments *without* providing alternative ideals, simply by revealing the *inconsistency* in our target positions. It is with this in mind that we move here from a later critic of Berlin's to one of his earlier liberal heroes, John Stuart Mill,[39] and in particular his most famous work of political philosophy, *On Liberty*. Here, Mill developed a very influential argument in favour of what we now call the 'harm principle', the idea that government can coerce individuals or groups only in order to stop them harming other individuals or groups. This way, he reasoned, each individual has as much freedom as is compatible with an equal freedom for others – or so Mill thought.

What then could be wrong with such an argument? Well, we might start off here by asking the following question: Why exactly *should* we place such value in this principle? To this, Mill might say, 'Well, why *not* place such value, given that it advances liberty, a clearly wonderful ideal?' Yet, if we look closely, we see of course that it is not just any kind of liberty. It is, to be precise, liberty of the same 'negative' kind that Berlin so admired. And why was that? In short, because Mill thought that maximising the sphere of personal choice, as he saw it, was good for individual self-development.[40] But here's the rub. Think carefully about how Mill's Victorian Britain worked, while also thinking about the fact that, if one ensures the harm principle, and no one is to be coerced unless they are harming someone else, then, as Mill is clear, no one can be coerced even to make them *help* someone else. And what does that mean? In short, there will be no redistributive taxation, as well as no restrictions on companies and individuals selling and advertising anything they like – sex,[41] opium,[42] thalidomide[43] – you name it.

This then raises an awkward question for Mill: just how good is this way of doing things going to be for the self-development of *most* people, including the very poor, the urban working class, and minorities of every kind? Unable even to verify what is in their bread,[44] and lacking any support if they fall on hard times, let alone state-funded healthcare and education, are they really as able as they *might* be to develop themselves into all that they *could* become? Clearly, Mill believes he has sketched out a world in which the harm principle protects our dearest form of liberty, with that form in turn valued for self-development, but is that really where his principle would naturally take us? Would it not, in truth, simply give us a world without redistributive taxation and in which people are, of course, 'safe' from governments, but without any protection from companies or con-artists? Or, put differently, isn't Mill's argument fundamentally *inconsistent*? That is, surely its aims fail to match its means, with the result being that the whole programme of political reform it *could* have inspired suddenly loses its attraction. If that's right, then, once again, critique, and in this case critique based on inconsistency, changes the way we look at our political options.

We have therefore, at this point, two forms of critique, each of which shows us how to tear down not just particular positions in political philosophy but also the political programmes they support. What then of our third form: 'suspicious roots'? Well, consider here that in the first case we looked for the problematic implications in either the assumptions or consequences of a given view, while in the second we looked for problems that emerge as a result of holding two or more incompatible commitments within it. By contrast, in this third option we focus not on the ideas themselves but on their origins.

Imagine, for example, that you had a real taste for alcohol but had alcoholic parents. What might knowing this fact do to you? Among other things, it might make you wary of where that taste came from, either through socialisation or unwelcome genes. *Uncovering* the origin of your taste, in other words, would *alter* your view of it. Or imagine you're a man who is so strong-minded that it means you always need to be the dominant partner in any relationship into which you enter. Perhaps you think that this is perfectly natural – even admirable, showing your true 'alpha-male' status – but maybe not. You might instead start to become suspicious of it if you also began to think it came from genes that made sense in a hunter-gatherer environment but not in a modern office environment – or indeed if it came from male role models who, in addition to encouraging your love of drink, also gave you a taste for domination. In both cases, then, the idea is the same – you become *suspicious* of your commitments not just in terms of where they might lead, or whether they are compatible with your other values and principles, but also in terms of where they have come from.

This form of critique has considerable *pedigree* in political theory – and I use that term deliberately, given that it highlights the exact opposite effect to what I have in mind, namely the idea that one might adhere to a particular commitment just because some wonderful, noble, clever, or revered figure was committed to it themselves: a prophet perhaps, or a national hero, or a feted theorist. By contrast, the idea here is that we *reject* an idea or set of ideas based on its history. Consider, for example, the following chain of reasoning derived from Marx – someone whom many have taken to be not just a great theorist but also some kind of prophet. This chain begins with his famous claim that 'the ideas of the ruling class are in every epoch the ruling ideas.'[45] For example, our 'ideas' regarding negative liberty do not simply follow on from Berlin or Mill, as key 'innovators' in our subject – they come at root from capitalism, an economic 'base' with an ideological 'superstructure'. And why is that? Well, the story goes something like this. Capitalism means competition, and competition means growth. Growth means new products, new markets, and an expansion of private property. This encourages colonialism in the first instance and globalisation in the second. It encourages the commodification of anything one can get one's hands on – or even just imagine, such as a derivative or patent. It encourages advertisements that constantly tell us how much we 'need' new things that we had never conceived of before, and so on and so forth. All of which leaves us with political ideals – liberal and individualistic, selfish and materialistic, cynical and unco-operative – that we might not find quite so animating once we know their origins.

This story, however, is not quite as one-sided as it seems, given that capitalism might *also* encourage things we take to be more straightforwardly positive. Perhaps, for example, it led to slavery becoming an inefficient mode of production – hence abolition. Perhaps the pressure of economic growth slowly brought women into the workplace – hence liberation. Perhaps the same has applied, over the years, for minority ethnic groups, sexualities, religions, and so on – leading to emancipation, political and economic, in every case. Perhaps then you would not put it as Marx did, when he wrote that the Jew in mid-nineteenth-century Germany did not get freedom from religion but freedom of religion, not freedom from property but freedom of property.[46] Instead, perhaps you would just think – Well, that's all to the good, so why complain? Or, at the least, why not just take the rough with the smooth?

Yet that is still not the full picture here. Building on the details of the story so far, the broader question it raises is this: What exactly should we think, or indeed *do*, when it turns out that our ideals stem from the interests of a system that is itself nobody's property, as well as nobody's plan? The answer, it seems, is this: surely we should start to worry about some of our most basic assumptions about human nature and its interests, including, say, your currently *cynical* view of our *potential* to co-operate *outside* of market trading. Rousseau, in this vein, once wrote of Hobbes that he confused human behaviour under tyranny for human behaviour in general,[47] while Diderot thought that *both* Hobbes and Rousseau simply generalised from the eras in which they lived – violent in Hobbes's case and peaceful in Rousseau's.[48] Here, in turn, we have a similar tale. Drawing on Marx, we have said that both modern capitalists and modern liberals take *human nature under capitalism*, in all its selfishness, materialism, and individualism, to be *human nature full stop*. And, of course, you might just want to say here that that's absolutely fine, given that you rather like this version of 'human nature' our modern world has produced. Yet you might alternatively say this: 'Now that I know how it came about, I certainly want to see if I can think up some better alternatives.' The point here then is simple: once this kind of history puts the 'naturalness' of certain ideas under suspicion, more things become possible, or at least imaginable, than would otherwise be the case.[49]

Now let's consider a second example of this kind of reasoning, this time from Nietzsche, and this time focused on the idea of 'genealogy'. As with Marx, the basic contention is the same. Although he doesn't think ideas flow from economic developments, he does think, again, that we should be wary of their origins, with Judaeo-Christian morality,[50] in this case, functioning as the villain of the piece. This story goes roughly as follows. When the Egyptians and then the Romans dominated the people of Judah, they developed a morality to cope with their domination that valorised the weak and downtrodden. This was a morality with roots in things such as the Fall from the Garden of Eden and Moses' Ten Commandments, but which really came to fruition, centuries later, with Christ's Sermon on the Mount, a treatise that expressed above all the idea that 'the meek shall inherit the earth'. That claim, thereafter, became the centrepiece of a world-view which, above all else, made us *guilty* for enjoying or even 'coveting' things that it tells us we should deny ourselves: domination, sport, sex, alcohol, and – who knows? – maybe even the rare and luxurious pleasure of political philosophy.

Are we then, for Nietzsche, trapped by this inheritance, by this move from the suffering of the few to the guilt of the many? Not at all, for there is also an equally historical alternative as expressed by the lives of the pre-Christian Greeks and Romans, as well as at least some pre-modern European aristocrats. Each of these groups, Nietzsche thought, had a much better idea of what counts as a fulfilling life,[51] whether that be in pursuit of 'Apollonian' practices, such as science or literature, or 'Dionysian' pleasures, such as sex, food, music, and so on. This alternative, however, is not the main story here. All that really matters is the force and nature of Nietzsche's *critical* point: that we should not be feeling *inherited* guilt about our personal ambitions, our taste for drink and sex, or even our love of artistic expression over 'useful' utilitarian labour, given that this misplaced sentiment stems from a dark and warped mind-set developed under domination. This, again, was the domination of Jews and then Christians, and in particular Christians who were first dominated by Rome, but who then took it over, spreading their ideology throughout the Roman Empire.[52] Or, as Nietzsche once put it, eventually the new Rome conquered the old,[53] just as the city's architectural centre shifted from the Senate to St Peter's.

So, if we zoom out again, what we have gathered here so far is this: two examples of 'suspicious roots' – one from Marx and one from Nietzsche – with both of them using historical scholarship in order to expose the supposedly troubling stories behind our most cherished beliefs. Yet that historical route is not the only one available to this form of critique. Taking our lead now from contemporary political theory, there is still another variant on 'suspicious roots' that merits our attention here. Consider, for example, Peter Singer's critique of Rawls and others when it comes to the 'naturalness' of some of our 'moral intuitions'.[54] Here the focus is on how we 'naturally' tend to prioritise, morally and politically speaking, those who are near and similar to ourselves – family, friends, compatriots, etc. – with the result that we now think it perfectly natural to divide the world into small democratic states with little in the way of obligations towards one another. As a consequence, we also find it difficult to deal with issues such as global poverty or climate change, because it's hard for us to see how much responsibility we could have to the rest of our species. Yet, for Singer, this is a great mistake. The 'naturalness' of our intuitions is not something we should just uncritically accept – any more than we should uncritically accept intuitions handed down to us by capitalism or Judaeo-Christian morality. Yes, a preference for those *similar* and *close* to us might have made sense when we spent most of our evolutionary history, as *Homo sapiens*, wandering around in small hunter-gatherer groups – but we don't live like that any more, do we?

# How?

As Singer explains it, some of our most basic moral and political instincts *only* really made sense in an environment that is now long gone – an environment in which no one group could ruin fish stocks, or global trade, or even the planet's climate, for everybody else. So where does that leave us now? Well, as with Nietzsche, the more general point of Singer's critique is simple: once we manage to see the origins of some of our core values in an *earlier situation*, and also see how that situation is *no longer ours*, then what we have done is to clear the way for a *new* position about how we should organise politics, without as yet *dictating that position*.

Or is that a bit too modest? Should we in truth say that, *whenever* power or forces beyond our control have played a hand in the origins of some of our ideas, that is *enough* to drive our choice for others in their place? Well, unfortunately not, as we'll see in a moment once we turn to the task of 'ordering'. This is because, as we have already seen, there are all kinds of reasons for us to accept or reject a given position, with only one coming from that position's history. After all, what if a position with a dubious history also happened to be the only position without *dangerous implications*? Or the only *consistent* position? And indeed, as for 'suspicious roots', so for our first two forms of critique. Positive liberty might well be a dangerous ideal, yet also one whose benefits can be safely enjoyed once it's penned in with an appropriate set of 'individual rights'. Mill's harm principle might be a great way of managing 'free speech', even if we choose not to roll it out more generally. And – who knows? – maybe none of evolution, Christianity, or even capitalism are *that* troubling once we've properly digested their historical descent. Sure, they might have changed who we are, but, having been changed, maybe we now like what we see.

For now, then, it is enough to conclude by saying, once again, that critique is a serious activity that comes in three different variants. No, it's not an answer to our subject's organising question, but it is certainly a contribution to one, as shown by the fact that it is the task to which most literature reviews, PhD theses, book reviews, and so on, are dedicated, as well as many articles and books. This is unsurprising, given that it's always on the basis of such 'critique' that we work closer to the kind of 'orderings' we are ultimately after, just as it's on the basis of our earlier 'analyses' that we mount such critiques.

## 3.4 Ordering

So far, we have seen how both analysis and critique work, with the former setting the targets and the latter pulling the trigger. This takes us to our third task, *ordering*. Here, as noted already, the aim is to build on our earlier analytical work by telling us exactly how to manage the problems and variables it reveals. Here, in turn, the aim is to build on earlier critical work by telling us exactly which answer to our subject's organising question should guide us, once all that critique is done. Yet how are we supposed to do that? How are we to know that we have found the right political position? How can we tell that we have done our ordering correctly?

Well, without prejudging the position we end up with, what we ultimately need is an ordering that meets at least two criteria.[55] First, it will have to be *convinc-*

*ing*, in the sense that whoever would have to live with it finds it more compelling than any of the alternatives. If I say to you, for example, to adopt communism because I happen to like the colour red, then I would expect you to wait for more compelling reasons. Second, it will have to be *meaningful*, in the sense that our answer is precise enough to give substantial guidance. If I say to you, for example, that we need a political system that ensures clean air or that avoids human extinction, then that is just too vague.

Why, though, do I use this odd term 'ordering' here, given that many would think 'arguments', 'theories', 'prescriptions', or 'visions' would work better? The reason is that none of those is quite right. One can have a theory of liberty, an argument about the origins of our view of liberty, or a vaguely liberal vision or prescription that is in no way precise or complete enough to give us the political guidance we need. Ordering, by contrast, with its connotations of *precision* and *priority*, keeps our eyes on the prize. In particular, it reminds us that simply saying, in this or that book or article, that we 'urgently' need to promote this or that value or principle is just not enough. One often sees this in our subject, yet collectively, if this is all we have, it gives us nothing more than a list of vaguely important values, problems, or principles. By contrast, in both the ideal world *and* the real world, we need to know how to rank our ambitions when not all such ambitions can be fully realised.[56] We need to know about our current world, not just that *x* is a shame or that introducing *y* would be nice, but also what would be, *all things considered*, a better *overall* way of organising things. We want, in other words – and this is another reason for using this term – an ordering that could define for us a *political order*.

We know, then, that we want to build on our analysis and critique by producing some kind of ordered vision that could tell us, convincingly and meaningfully, *how we should live*. We also know, from earlier discussions, that this ordering needs to take the form of a principle or set of principles that achieves this aim by telling us just how to deal with various problems and manage various variables. But, again, how are we to produce this? How are we to argue about such things? How are we to know that one ordering is more convincing than another and, indeed, that it is sufficiently meaningful?

The standard way to do it is via something I call *mentalism*.[57] This is a way of working out how to order a set of principles by figuring out those principles to which we are *already* committed, even if we are as yet *unaware* of them and even if that means *eliminating* some of our political commitments along the way. At root, this means practising a kind of introspection, or 'thinking about thinking', according to which, and in similar fashion to some of the conceptual analysis practised above, we explore our thoughts and feelings about this or that situation, this or that value, or this or that problem, in order to see just which principles we end up affirming. Or, even more precisely, which principles we end up affirming 'upon reflection', where 'upon reflection' means precisely the kind of exploration just described. These principles, crucially, would be *ours* in the sense that they already *buried*, and then *discovered*, in our thinking, even though, as discussed above, theorists refine and *innovate* around them in the process. As a result, they are convincing to us precisely because they are principles to which we already roughly adhere, with the attendant hope being that they are also meaningful enough to provide a precise and ordered answer to our organising question.

Yet how exactly do we do this kind of introspection? Essentially we have a process composed of two steps: *extraction* and *elimination*.[58] The first, *extraction*, is what we do when we try to *derive* principles from our 'normative thoughts' – thoughts about what should and should not be the case in the world and what we should and should not do within it.[59] These thoughts are the rocks out of which we extract the ore of our principles, and they in turn come in three forms, all of which need to be borne in mind – no pun intended – as material we might want to work with.

The first of these is 'impartial choices of ideal state': choices made regarding an answer to our organising question in situations defined by rules regarding what we know of ourselves and the world, the nature of which is hopefully such that we both *accept* these rules and all make the *same* choice. One example of such a choice is the selection of principles of justice Rawls thinks we would make in his famous 'original position', in which we are denied various bits of information about ourselves, such as our race, class, or sex. We are supposed to accept this situation because we accept, broadly speaking, the idea that choices of political principles should not be biased by certain factors, including not just our wealth and race but even our tastes and talents.

Second, we have 'considered judgements'. These are judgements that experienced and informed individuals are supposed to share about various social, economic, and political processes and institutions. Consider, for example, the conviction that 'slavery is wrong' or that 'political positions shouldn't be automatically closed to ethnic minorities'. The appeal of these judgements lies both in how widely shared they are and in how strongly we hold them.

Finally we have our third type: 'intuitive choices of abstract principle'. These are non-inferential choices made in hypothetical scenarios in which our decisions are somehow supposed to reveal and express our principles. Singer, for example, once asked us to imagine whether or not we would save a child drowning in a pond next to us if we could do so at little cost to ourselves and assumed, quite rightly, that we would do so. On the basis of that presumed hypothetical decision, he then inferred that we are, by extension, intuitively committed to the principle 'save lives when you can do so at little cost to yourself'.[60] Situations like these are what we often call 'thought experiments'[61] – as are certain 'impartial choices of ideal state' – and they are called that in the sense that we ask ourselves, or others, what we would intuitively do or not do in a given situation, with the 'data' revealed by those 'experiments' coming in the form not just of these instinctive decisions but ultimately of principles those decisions are supposed express.

We have, then, three types of thought that we can use for extraction, and thus as our core material when trying to work out the principles to which we are *already committed* in virtue of the way we *already think*. Consider, for example, the following thought experiment. Your neighbour lends you a gun and you promise to return it at 2 p.m. tomorrow. Just before that time comes, you hear him shout at his wife that he is going to kill her, and a moment later he knocks on your door, asking for the gun's return. What do you do? Most of us say 'Keep the gun and call the police'. If so, then it seems to follow, in virtue of how we think about this situation, that we favour the principle 'prevent harm' over the principle 'keep your promises'. This then gives us a reason to prioritise that principle out in the real world. Or imagine you work for the coastguard and can save one sinking boat but not two. The first has ten passengers and the second thirty. Again, what do you do? Well, you probably save the one with thirty, in which case it looks like you're committed to a principle such as 'always save the greatest number'. What we are doing here then, once again, is looking for principles to which we are already committed in virtue of the thoughts we already have. Whether looking at the first, second, or third of the three types of thought set out a moment ago, we are trying to find the principles expressed or entailed by those thoughts, just as natural scientists look for laws in, say, the movements of planets or the formation of clouds.[62]

There is, however, a problem with all this extraction when it comes to ordering, which is that we rapidly end up with more principles than we know what to do with. Consulting your own thoughts, you might readily see that one considered judgement takes you this way, a separate intuitive choice of abstract principle takes you that way, and a separate choice of ideal state takes me another way. We encounter, therefore, the problem that many of our normative thoughts are incompatible, especially once we realise that most can be pursued *ad infinitum* and thus at the expense of your other concerns.

I can, for example, pursue both security and equality but cannot put limitless resources into both. I can dream of both equality and liberty yet might soon find, as did the Jacobins, that they very quickly compete with one another.

It is with this problem in mind that we now bring our second stage of the process into play: *elimination*. This is a key stage for us, bearing in mind that our broader aim here, with 'ordering', is of course to try and *eliminate* all but one set of principles, and thus all but one way of ordering them – leaving us with just *one* answer to our subject's 'organising question'. In other words, channelling Karl Popper, rather than just trying to show that *one* such answer is a good answer we also need to *falsify* all the alternative answers. And, indeed, we might even go as far as John Stuart Mill, who once remarked that, in matters like these, 'three-quarters' of our arguments must be arguments against either alternatives or objections to our own position – as opposed to just arguments directly in our favour.[63] Or, put differently again, we might think that 'three-quarters' of our argument in pursuit of a particular ordering, if Mill is right, would be dedicated to the task we are calling elimination. And that's an interesting rule of thumb here, given that, as a matter of fact, it is if anything exceeded by the general spread of scholarship in political philosophy, which devotes *at least* three-quarters of its attention to critical engagement with rival positions.

Again, though, how do we actually do this? In short, by doing precisely the kind of critique we discussed in the previous section, though now with one key addition, given that, at this stage, we are interested in claims of 'dangerous implications', 'inconsistency', and 'suspicious roots' not just as a means of undermining various values and principles but also as a means of undermining particular *orderings* of such things. That is, we are interested in critiquing not just *isolated* arguments, focused on particular values or principles, but also the arguments that seek to *tie them all together* into particular political orders, and thus particular answers to our organising question. For example, we are now interested not just in H. L. A. Hart's critique of Rawls's 'basic liberties' principle,[64] the first principle he thinks we would choose in his 'original position', but also Philippe Van Parijs's critique of the 'lexical' ordering of the three principles that emerge in total,[65] according to which one maximises the first before the second and the second before the third (though Rawls always described the second and third as two parts of a single principle). Or, less esoterically, we are now interested not just in whether this or that thinker has properly nailed down this or that concept, or properly set up this or that thought experiment, but also whether the overall political order they have in mind – assuming they have one – is just the sort of thing we should be turning into political reality.

This small 'addition', then, is simply a shift in focus, meaning that there's no need to go over old ground here as regards the nature of the three kinds of critique – for we know well enough at this point how they work. As explained, one scholar simply argues with another that their values, principles, or even ordering of principles, have dangerous implications, or are in some way inconsistent, or have suspicious roots. There is, however, one further and important tactic here that was not mentioned earlier but which becomes more salient when addressing arguments about an ordering of principles as an answer to our subject's organising question. This is the tactic of, in effect, converting *facts* into *feasibility objections*: that is, the utilisation of various facts about the world in order to label particular orderings of principles as hopelessly infeasible, or utopian, and so on. Now, admittedly, that term 'utopian' does tell us just how close we are to the first form of critique considered earlier – dangerous implications – yet there is an important difference here. Before we might only have been saying that an ideal is *dangerous*, whereas now we are saying it's *impossible*. Of course, that might not entirely ruin the appeal of the ideal in question – we might just say that it provides a gold standard, or yardstick, against which all second-best efforts can be measured in the real world, provided it's true that the closer to it we get the better. Yet when it comes to comparing different orderings of principles, feasibility certainly matters. That one ordering is much more feasible than another would be, all things considered, a very good reason for choosing it.

Do notice here, though, that this use of feasibility is also part and parcel of mentalism more generally, as discussed so far, and is not some sort of practical appendage I have fixed to the side. This is because even this form of critique relies upon a thought we are *assumed* to hold already: that we should not say that something *should* be the case, in politics or elsewhere, unless it *could* be the case. We do not, for example, think a father is a bad father if he does not put the moon on a stick for his son, however much he asks for it. Nor do we think that a government is a bad government if it has not yet eliminated all unhappiness, or failed relationships, or unreciprocated love, and so on.

# How?

Such thoughts are normally distilled by philosophers into the principle 'ought-implies-can', and when applied to the task of elimination, as noted, that principle is a powerful weapon. We might, for example, rule out the socialist principle 'from each according to their capacity, to each according to their need' on the basis that it is incompatible with human nature. Or we might reject a particular vision of 'deliberative democracy', given that it assumes levels of political engagement, emotional detachment, and even information that are infeasible in the world both as we know it and as we know it could be. And so it goes on. In each case, we might just say that, because we *cannot* achieve such things, we *ought not* to pursue them.

Let's get back here, though, to our main focus. Remember: what we are trying to do here when pursuing an 'ordering' of principles, and thus a convincing and meaningful answer to our 'organising question', is justify one particular ordering via *extraction* while *falsifying* all others via *elimination*. That, in essence, is our task. So far, we have seen broadly how this extraction and elimination is supposed to work, taking our own thoughts as the key material with which to work and argue, and building on the kind of analysis and critique discussed so far in this chapter. There is, however, more flexibility to this process than might be apparent from all these claims, and in at least three dimensions.

First, the ordering we end up with could be *universal* and *timeless* – the right one for all people at all times – or just *local* and *contemporary* – fit for twenty-first-century Germans but of little purchase on, say, twelfth-century Mongols. Second, it could be more or less idealistic. As explained, an ordering could be more or less feasible, given that we sometimes want to use ideals as benchmarks, or lodestars, against which we measure ourselves. They can be, in Plato's phrase, something we root in our heart, or see in the stars, despite our never quite realising them.[66] Third, and this connects back to an earlier comment about the collective nature of political philosophy's mission, just because we are after a convincing and meaningful ordering of principles we should not expect any one theorist to do all the relevant work. Of course, we have a problem if each theorist simply preaches their own values and principles without either producing an ordering or engaging with the rival views of others, but not if they work together in order to iron out the final picture.

This in turn gives us a more general point: whether or not our orderings are universal or particular, idealistic or fully realisable, and individually or collectively established – all of this, again, *ultimately depends on the content of the normative thoughts we work with*. How much do they vary? How demanding are they? How numerous and complicated are they? We won't know, really, *until we look*, meaning that ambitions have to be tailored to results. For example, if (most) Americans agree with one another in (most of) their deepest normative thoughts while disagreeing with (most) non-Americans, then that's fine, we can work with that. Or, if we *all* agree on abstract principles but not on considered judgements, then again, that's fine, and we'll work with it. Or, if we agree on democracy but *not* on the details of justice, then, again, we could still accept that while producing some kind of convincing and meaningful answer to our organising question for at least some relevant political group.

There are, though, some interesting possible implications to this point regarding the different ways in which our orderings might vary, starting with the way they might affect the processes of extraction and elimination described. Consider here, for example, that one might render these processes much more sophisticated by talking, as Rawls does, of *reflective equilibrium*, *wide reflective equilibrium*, and *general reflective equilibrium*.[67] The first of these holds that one arrives at one's answer to our organising question by studying our thoughts in order to see what principles they mostly support, and then assessing those remaining thoughts in order to see whether to revise either them or the principles, and *then* going on in that fashion until one has a perfect equilibrium between thoughts and principles. The second, *wide reflective equilibrium*, says that one undertakes this same process not just in the light of one's own thinking but also in light of all the many arguments one finds throughout political philosophy more generally, as this way one is exposed to as many candidate principles as possible and also as many critiques as one can muster. The third, *general reflective equilibrium*, suggests finally that we should be aiming for a state of affairs whereby everyone in society arrives at the same political position via wide reflective equilibrium.[68]

Now, one possible implication of these variants is this: if each of these three counts as a plausible version of the kind of argument described so far in this section, we might face the problem that each pulls in a different political direction, depending on how many views, or indeed how many individuals, they include in the pursuit of our 'ordering'. Yet this should not unduly worry us here, and for at least three reasons. First, because the obvious choice here would be for 'wide' reflective equilibrium over the first kind mentioned, given that we have long been discussing not just reflection upon our own thoughts but also reflection upon *the best arguments available to us* – including the best analyses, critiques, and orderings available to us – as produced by others. If I want a medical diagnosis, for example, I will not rely purely upon my own reasoning – I will draw on as many expert views as possible. And, indeed, what would be the point of political philosophy, or indeed of politics, if it began and ended with myself, with no detour in between?

Second, as regards a choice between the second and third kind, if the issue is of *how many people* need to be convinced by an ordering in order for it to be the one that I should adopt, then that will depend on who those people are, where they live, what other orderings might potentially convince them, and so on and so forth. As stated a moment ago, we cannot pre-judge this process. We cannot limit, in advance, either the detail or the scale of the political order we are trying to identify.[69] I still have to consult my own thoughts and the best arguments available, as only then will I know exactly with whom I need to align in terms of my settled political view.

Third, and this is the most important point of all, for us even to adopt a particular 'method' for identifying a particular ordering, whether reflective equilibrium in one of its guises or something else altogether, we need first of all to be sure that it expresses, as with everything else, *principles to which we already adhere*. In other words, such 'methods' are subordinate to everything we have said already about extraction, elimination, and so on. Or, put differently, I cannot adopt a particular method for ordering my commitments unless I'm already sure that it in some way reflects at least some of those commitments.

Consider then here, with this key point in mind, some of the further and plausible options currently available in political philosophy as regards how we might methodologically narrow our pursuit of a particular ordering. We might, for example, and as already noted, choose to restrict ourselves to thoughts and arguments found *locally* and *currently*, in which case we might talk here not of 'reflective equilibrium' but of 'contextualism'.[70] In this case we would be working out 'how we should live' for a particular context, as defined by a particular group of people – national, religious, cultural, or even just those living in a particular era. Or we might follow Alasdair MacIntyre and put more weight on the comparison of rival traditions of argument, such as 'Aristotelianism', or what he calls 'The Enlightenment Project'.[71] In this case, although our ambitions might be more universalistic, we would be arguing for a contemporary answer to the question 'How should we live?' based simply on the best arguments that human beings have come up with so far, while acknowledging that better ones might come along in the future. Or, as a third example, we might do all of this via Socratic dialogue and set up a continuous adversarial argument regarding analysis, critique, and various rival orderings of principles in order to see where one ends up. In this case we would be hoping that the innovative ideas that emerge as a result of exchange are better than those that started it all off.

Once more, though, however one does it, the basic idea in play is the same. Whatever body of scholarly argument we draw upon as a way of alerting us to new problems, values, principles, orderings, and so on, we always work at a fundamental level with the *thoughts we already have*, meaning that we use them both as resources out of which we extract possibilities and as materials for the elimination of, hopefully, all but one of those possibilities. As a result, we might then wonder: Is there no alternative to what I have called mentalism? Well, perhaps not. Given that justification will always be *by* someone, *of* something, and *to* someone else, it seems sensible to think that we can justify a particular ordering to anyone *only* in virtue of commitments they *already have*, however *buried* or *inchoate* they are, and even if that means their *abandoning* whichever commitments are currently incompatible with what they ultimately come to realise are their *chief*, or *core*, or most *crucial* ones.

There is, however, one partial alternative to this way of doing things, which is worth noting here if only further to clarify the orthodoxy. This is an odd method or model of justification that I call 'normative behaviourism',[72] and its key claim is this: we should argue for a set of principles on the basis that they are the principles people prefer not upon reflection but, rather, *in practice*, as revealed by the *behaviour* of billions of people over hundreds and maybe thousands of years. I said earlier that we normally use 'facts' as materials for feasibility objections, yet clearly for normative behaviourism they also have a second use. Consider, for example, Adam Przeworski's empirical finding that no democracy with a GDP per capita more than that of Argentina in 1976 (roughly $4,000) has ever collapsed.[73] Consider the Polity Project's claim that democracies are more stable than any other historically tested political regime.[74] And consider Wilkinson and Pickett's claim that the more inequality you have, the more crime you get.[75] Normative behaviourism says that facts like these show what people are committed to *once they have to live with different systems*, with those systems in turn understood as expressions of different *orderings of principles*. It is these commitments based on *experience* that matter (including the experience of others, whom we treat as equivalent to ourselves) and not armchair reflections on what we *imagine* we might like or do, including in situations we hope are somehow analogous to this or that aspect of politics, such as children drowning in ponds.

Again, though, I do not push for this position here, and even if I did it also would not change our key point, which is, once more, that even when adopting an unusual method like this, in pursuit of a particular ordering to guide our way, we still cannot do anything that has no appeal to *us*, in virtue of the commitments we *already hold*. So, even if we were to pay more attention to actions rather than thoughts, there would still need to be *reasons* that make sense to *us*, in terms of what *already* matters to us, that could steer us in that direction.

As a result, the best reason for exploring these different methods is simply that they provide a proper sense of the variety of arguments available to us. None of them alters the character of our central mission with this third task of 'ordering', which is, one last time, as follows: we *order* when we provide a convincing argument that one meaningful political principle – or set of principles – is somehow better than another as an answer to our subject's organising question: How should we live? This, at root, is what we aim to do, in political philosophy, when arguing that a principle is the right principle for us, or the most rational, or the most reasonable. It is also something we do both when extracting options from our thoughts (or behaviour) and when eliminating them down using that very same material. We hope, of course, that the picture that emerges is widely shared among at least a single population, if not humanity as a whole, just as we hope that it is detailed enough to offer substantial political guidance, but we know that it is *only a hope*, before the games begin. We will not know for sure until we have looked as hard as we can.

### 3.5 Conclusions

The point of this chapter has been to set out the three core tasks followed by political philosophers in pursuit of our subject's organising question. As noted, this means one could describe the 'point' of political philosophy more generally as simply being to try and answer that question. Yet that still doesn't fully cover it. Among other things, saying that this is our aim wouldn't explain why we write what we write in the way that we write it, or in the places we publish it. As a result, the 'point' of the next chapter is to explore not just the wider purpose behind our trying to answer our subject's organising question but also the rationale behind the way we currently engage, in our work, both with one another and with the wider world.

# 4
# Why?

## 4.1 Introduction

This chapter explores three goals one might have in mind when *doing* political philosophy, in the sense of thinking and writing about it. These run as follows. First, I might do it out of intellectual curiosity – the ideas fascinate me, and I like playing around with them. Second, I might do it in order to figure out my own political orientations – I'm confused or conflicted about various issues and need philosophical reasoning to point me in the right direction. Third, I might do it in order to make the world a better place – having figured out what I think ought to be the case in politics, I now want to protect and promote those ideas out there in the 'real world'. Over the course of this chapter, I discuss each of these goals in turn, with special attention paid to that third idea of making the world a better place, given the careful discussion it requires of the relationship between scholars and, respectively, politicians, movements, and even students. An overarching conclusion for the chapter, and indeed the book as a whole, as long noted, is that there are clearly many reasons for doing political philosophy, all of which are perfectly valid and all of which could be in play at the same time, and for the same individual. A second conclusion, less obvious but just as urgent, is that, because ideas always matter in politics, political philosophy always has the potential for serious influence. If it does not exert that influence, then other producers of ideas – whether gurus and columnists or scientists and economists – will simply fill the gap themselves.

## 4.2 Intrinsic interest

We start then with intellectual curiosity, or, put differently, the idea that political philosophy is just *intrinsically interesting* – that is, interesting for its own sake and not just for some wider purpose it might serve. This is unsurprising, given that the universe in general is an interesting place. It is, for example, interesting to know how stars and planets are formed and where our galaxy comes from, even when it's of no practical use to find out. It's interesting to know how other humanoids, such as Neanderthals, died off, even if we never saw how they lived. It's even interesting, turning back to philosophy, to know just how *hard* it is really to *know* what it's like to be a bat,[1] even when you can't become batman. Clearly, there is much to fascinate us, from the art forms of dead civilisations to the mating habits of bower birds. Clearly, we are curious creatures with much to be curious about, including ourselves, but also political philosophy.

# Why?

Consider here all the different ways in which political philosophy intrigues us, including those connected to that more general quest of getting to know oneself. For example, it's interesting simply to know *how we should live*, even if you never tell anybody, and no one ever asks. That is, it's rewarding just to have *figured out* how politics *should* work, even if no one ever makes you queen or emperor, just as it's rewarding to solve a particularly tricky crossword or sudoku puzzle. Similarly, it's interesting to weigh up different political principles and orderings thereof, even if you never agree with them, and especially so when it casts your own principles in a new light. Contemplating, say, the socialist principle of 'from each according to their capacity, to each according to their need', and thinking about how that principle might play out in the real world, is fascinating stuff. We might, for example, imagine how it can work in a family setting, where each member helps where they can and does what they are best able to do. Or we might think about how it could regulate the life of a whole nation, or even a global political and economic order. In doing so, we will be struck by where it seems to work easily, where it seems impossible, and where we just wouldn't know until we tried.

For related reasons, it's also interesting to contemplate the different visions expressed by works as distant, and as daring, as Plato's *Republic*. Here it doesn't matter if we never want to live in a world in which we are divided into three classes, told myths about why people belong in such classes, told to avoid such dangerous things as Corinthian girlfriends and Syracusan cookery, and even told to embrace naked gymnastics. It just doesn't matter if that sounds, as it must, outlandish or indulgent to us, because it's still wonderful just to *imagine* it at all, and of course to see the surprising ways in which it both *differs from* and *resembles* our contemporary status quo, as well as our ideals for changing it. It is, in other words, interesting to explore politico-philosophical ideas, both radical and conservative, even if one never puts them into practice. Or, put differently, it's interesting to do political philosophy even if you never do the politics, just as it's interesting to play war games even if you never fight a war, and just as it is interesting, though far from ideal, to write a book that nobody reads.

## 4.3 Individual guidance

Nonetheless, even if intrinsic interest is one good reason for doing political philosophy, it is certainly not the only reason. Sure, it can be a *sufficient* reason for lots of people, but there are other possible reasons too. Consider here, for example, how some go to church, mosque, or synagogue for the feel of community, some for fear of death, some because of the social mission on offer, some out of hope and compassion, some out of guilt and fear, and some because they just believe. Some of these individuals do so for one of these reasons and others for several of them, yet there is no one reason covering everyone's motivation. It's that way with most things, including political philosophy. We might be acting out of intrinsic interest, but we might also be acting in pursuit of something else. What then might be a second reason for doing political philosophy, beyond the sheer intellectual buzz of it all?

Let's focus here on the case of the individual – someone who reads political philosophy and maybe even writes about it for some or other audience. What's in it for them, besides intrinsic interest? Well, one obvious motivation would be to look for guidance for their actions, even where 'actions' boils down to nothing more than the choice of where to cast their vote. You might, for example, be struggling to choose between candidates, parties, or policies, whether in local elections or national referenda. How do you make this decision? We might say, 'Consult your own *interests* – which one makes you better off?' Perhaps you have student loans to service and are tempted by the party offering to cancel them. Or perhaps you are retired and looking to maximise your pension. This is certainly one way of coming to a decision, though, for most of us, most of the time, it won't be the whole story or even the main story. Our 'interests', under normal circumstances, come down to more than just money in our pocket. We also want governments to promote our *values*, and we worry about how the world or even just our nation or local community looks and behaves. We care about whether national parks are created and protected, about whether 'faith schools' expand or shrink, and about whether taxes flow more to the disabled, or refugees, or public-sector workers. We care about whether we're set to become a fairer, freer, happier, safer society or not. We care about whether we go to war or not, and about the institutions and electoral systems that govern that decision. All of these are issues that fall outside our own narrow, material interest, and all of these, crucially, require us to work out the principles that we think ought to regulate the world – that define *how we live*. These are the principles which, *for us*, would advance the right kind of freedom, enhance our safety, and get us all behaving in ways in which, upon reflection, we think we ought to behave. And this, of course, is the business of political philosophy: figuring out the principles we want to see expressed in the world; arguing about those principles; and providing materials through which individuals can orientate themselves in the face of confusion, complexity, and conflict.

One might then describe this part of political philosophy's *raison d'être* as follows. Although most of us, most of the time, would *like* the world to be a better place, most of us, most of the time, are *unsure* about what that involves. And note, we are unsure not just in terms of, say, which politicians to *trust* or whether this or that macro-economic policy will generate *economic growth* – the questions that usually dominate the news agenda – but also in terms of which priorities and thus principles we ought to pursue. We are unsure, for example, whether to distribute political power to cities, regions, countries, continents, or the world at large. We do not know whether the world should have one thousand countries, one hundred, or just one. We do not know how much inequality is OK, and indeed of what kind.

Consider, for example, that, if one person chooses to spend their life surfing and another beavers away at their desk, dreaming of the beach beyond their window but denying themselves that dream in pursuit of long-term dividends, then presumably the resultant inequality is nothing to worry about. What, though, if someone never has the financial means to go into higher education or start a business, though they have the ability and dedication to do it? Maybe then we should raise taxes to help people in that latter situation, and perhaps via progressive taxation – more from the rich and less from the poor. How can we do that, though, without taking too much liberty from the contributors and instilling too much dependence in the recipients? After all, why work if it will be taxed, and why not surf, instead of working, if you're going to be helped anyway?

Again, then, because we *worry* about such issues, and because they fail to yield *easy* answers, we should be glad that political philosophy is *devoted* to them and could help us if given a chance. Yet that doesn't mean our level of interest is constant. As it happens, the more political philosophy we absorb, the more we come to see the importance and difficulty of these problems, meaning that our appreciation of the subject only grows the more we engage with it, in some cases leading to full-blown inspiration. You might, for example, find yourself tempted by communism, having read Marx and Engels's *The Communist Manifesto*, or by more moderate socialism, having read G. A. Cohen's final piece of work, *Why not Socialism?* You might be led to libertarianism, or something like neoliberalism, having read Nozick's *Anarchy, State, and Utopia* or, again, something more moderate such as Jason Brennan's response to the work by Cohen just mentioned – in his case entitled *Why not Capitalism?*

Maybe, having read David Miller's *Strangers in our Midst*, you decide that the social-democratic state in which you live is a wonderful thing, just as it is, and needs protecting with robust border controls. Or maybe, having read Carens's *The Ethics of Immigration*, you decide that open borders and uninhibited human movement are the way to go. And then where do you turn? Well, perhaps, when worried about contemporary politics, you click on a talk online by Martha Nussbaum on the place of emotions such as fear and anger in contemporary politics.[2] Perhaps you come across the work of Amy Gutmann and Dennis Thompson and decide that what this fearful and angry world really needs is a new spirit of compromise.[3] Or perhaps you start watching Michael Sandel's introductory lectures as a way to understand better all of the above.[4] All the while you find yourself welling up with ideas, inspiration, and indignation. All the while you learn from scholars who have spent their *life* thinking about the things that often already worry you and who have read everything they can find by other people who have spent *their* life thinking about such questions. So, even when you don't agree with them – and that is perfectly normal – they can still help you find your path, bearing in mind that each of us works out our political views not just by replication but also by differentiation.

## 4.4 Societal benefits

What, though, is the *cumulative* effect of such work? Does it make the world a better place? Does it make societies happy and peaceful? Or does it just make them more divided, angrier, ideological places in which every compromise is somehow ugly and no one ever gets a system even close to what they think we ought to have? This is a serious worry, given that online politics in general, and recent American politics in particular, fits that last description all too well. Increasingly, we live in a world of ideological *enemies* in which each side is regularly *outraged* by the *extremes* of its rivals. And all this despite – or is it because of? – ever higher levels of education. What then would it mean to add political philosophy, or at least more political philosophy, to this mix? Would it not be the equivalent of free cocaine at 'kicking out' time on a British high street on Saturday night? Would it not just encourage, particularly in the minds of the young and radical, of *both* left and right, overconfidence, hyper-aggression, and an insatiable level of entitlement?

Perhaps, then, our position here, channelling Plato, and contrary to the aims of this book, should be to say that philosophy must be kept purely for older and more disciplined minds, given this risk of encouraging dangerous sophistry in the young. Or, perhaps more modestly, and this time channelling Churchill – though the phrasing has older and murkier roots – we should say that, sure, if you don't think about political philosophy in your twenties, then you have no heart, but, please, if you don't put it to one side in your thirties, then you have no head. Either way, on this account, society needs to be on its guard when it comes to political philosophy, given that encouraging it would only be fanning the flames of a fire we do not want. Clearly, if everybody's a utopian, then nobody's happy. Or, more worryingly, and remembering Berlin from the last chapter, if everybody's a utopian, then potentially everybody's a dangerous revolutionary. As examples, we might say that, from Marx, we get Marxists, followed by Soviet gulags; from Rousseau, Jacobins, followed by the terrors of the French Revolution. This would make the political weather forecast, whenever political philosophy is prominent, something like 'unhappiness with a chance of violence'. It would also make Burke right when he described our subject, as noted earlier, as one that puts 'gallows at the end of every vista'.

Fearful pessimism, therefore, is clearly *one* response, and also one rather *plausible* response, to the prospect of a society richly informed by political philosophy. Yet it's not the *only* response. In truth, a society in which political philosophy is properly practised and disseminated should be better off, in all sorts of ways, even if not a single grand 'ordering', as propounded by any particular political philosopher, is put into place.

This becomes clear once we think back to the tasks of analysis and critique discussed in the previous chapter, as well as their culmination in the task of ordering. Through analysis, even if we don't all agree on what perfection would involve, we at least come to see with clarity what our options are, eliminating muddled or confused positions along the way. Through critique, in turn, we learn of reasons to be wary of some or indeed all of those options, and thus gain an initial set of reasons regarding how to rank, prioritise, curtail, or even eliminate some of those options. Through ordering, finally, by considering different arguments for different overall positions, as made up of different prioritisations and as defined by different sets of principles, we better understand the overall coherence of our political positions, including their implications for political practice. All of which means that, even if what we end up with, in reality, is a muddy compromise between such orderings, and even if no one is perfectly happy with it, it is at least a better compromise than we would have had in the absence of political philosophy, given the way it's been informed by *clearer* ideas, *stronger* critiques, and more *coherent* orderings.

But does this *really* make for a happier and more peaceful society? Well, yes, and for at least two reasons. First, because it renders us much more likely to avoid political programmes which, when properly assessed, increase the chances of *unhappiness* and *conflict*. That will be central to what we uncover via analysis, critique, and ordering. Second, because it is also part of the job of political philosophy, as part of these three tasks, to work out just what *kind* of peace and *what* kind of happiness it is that we *really* want to protect and pursue. After all, dictators often manage to deliver peace through fear, while some kinds of happiness, despite first appearances, are simply euphoria before the comedown. Or consider the related and politically significant idea of *development*. Here we might ask: How are we to develop ourselves, let alone help other countries develop, unless we know exactly what it is we ought to be aiming at? With this in mind, we might point to the case of Amartya Sen, the political philosopher and Nobel Prize-winning economist, who in 2012 was awarded the National Humanities Medal by President Barack Obama. He received this award for, *inter alia*, his work on producing the UN's favoured measure of development – the Human Development Index (HDI) – and his citation for this award captures our point here well: 'By applying philosophical thinking to questions of policy, he has changed how standards of living are measured.'[5]

So, it's clearly in our interest to realise, via political philosophy, just what *kind* of peace, happiness, development, and so on, we should be aiming for, and even what kind we have already *achieved*, as perhaps then we will start to see things such as 'online conflict' among the

young and radical, as mentioned earlier, as an achievement, given the physical alternatives – or at least as
an unavoidable by-product of a freedom we would not
want to lose. Maybe, for example, it is something akin
to what Engels had in mind when he described votes as
'paper stones'[6] – his point being that democracy, for all
its vices, is at least a more peaceful way of having an
argument than war. As a result, we might just say that,
if things such as conflict and unhappiness are things we
want to avoid, and if things such as peace and happiness
are things we want to both understand and promote,
then why *wouldn't* you want to encourage an activity
that considers such things, and which tries to tell us
which set of ordered principles best promotes them?

Again, then, political philosophy makes for more
informed choices, fewer errors, and hopefully more of
whatever it is we end up wanting once we've thought
enough about whatever it is that might be. Yet that is
still not quite the end of our story here. There are still,
as it happens, at least two key ideas we need to add
to the mix, both of which have been amply studied
and disseminated by political philosophers. These are,
respectively, 'deliberative democracy' and 'free speech',
and to see their significance we should start off by considering how an apparently *non*-political process works:
trial by jury. What, then, we might wonder, is the key
idea behind this practice? It is, at root, the assumption
that, as you increase the number of people responsible
for making a judgement, you increase the likelihood of
that judgement being correct. This is famously captured
in Condorcet's 'jury theorem', according to which we
need to believe only that each individual has a greater
than $0.5$ chance of being correct for the odds of getting a

correct verdict to improve as the number of jurors rises.[7] So what does that tell us about politics? Presumably it tells us that the more people we have involved in *political* decision-making, as opposed to legal verdicts, the better our decisions will be, even if each us is barely more accurate than the toss of a coin. Of course, that need not mean mass discussion and oversight of every choice, but it does give us a *prima facie* reason to encourage democracy – though not *yet* political philosophy.

In order to see where political philosophy comes in, think now in terms not of *people* but of *ideas*, and consider here, with this in mind, a new argument from Mill's *On Liberty*, in this case concerning 'free speech'. At root, his case is as follows: unless society enjoys relatively unlimited discussion, new ideas will not be advanced, while good ideas will not be defended, including old ones that are no longer subject to critique, with the consequence being that support for them ebbs away, dwindling along with the understanding that brought them into being.[8] As a result, not only does *progress* in the world of ideas fail to happen, but *regression* becomes likely. And, as for ideas, so for democratic politics, given that democracy, after all, is not just about *counting* votes and then making decisions but also about the *deliberations* that precede those counts.

That is, in order for 'the people' to make their choice, they need to know their options, and ideally they would see those options presented to them first shaped by a prior process of back and forth argument rather than just emerging from a smoke-filled room. All of which means several things for our topic here. It means that a society with access to lots of ideas does better than one with access to few. It means that a society that hears arguments for and against those ideas does better than one without such exchange. It means that, just as we get better political choices with more voters, so do we get better choices with more ideas and arguments, making 'free speech' and the 'deliberative' aspect of a functioning democracy crucial. Think here, for example, of how a greater choice of ingredients makes for a better meal, a greater choice of partners for a better marriage, a greater choice of clothes for a better fit, and a greater choice of destinations for a better holiday. In similar vein, the more options we know about in politics, and the more arguments we are exposed to about their nature, as well as their pros and cons, the better off our politics will be.

So, political philosophy, as a production factory of ideas and arguments, should in theory make society better off. And maybe not just in theory. Perhaps we could say that at least *some* of what we have described played at least *some* role in the relatively happy place we have reached today in at least *some* parts of the world. If, for example, philosophically informed political argument was part of the process that took the United Kingdom from the rule of a king to the rule of a parliament, which took that parliament from approval of slavery and restricted votes to approval of abolition and universal suffrage, and which kept that parliament strong during both the fight against fascism and the birth of the welfare state, then why wouldn't a society want more of it? Or, more grandly still, if these processes have played a similar role around the world, from the American Constitution to the Haitian revolution, then why wouldn't every society want it?

## 4.5 Theorists and politicians

Unfortunately, despite the logic of this route from theory to practice, and despite these latter allusions to historical progress, we still might be a little sceptical here and say, 'Sure, we can easily paint a rosy picture in which ivory tower and political power talk happily and productively all day long, but has this *really* ever happened, and, if so, precisely *how* does it happen?' That is, how exactly are new ideas and arguments disseminated and encouraged or discouraged in the world? And what examples are there of it ever having happened to date?

Well, let's start with that second question, regarding real-life cases, and then work our way up to the logistics involved. And, indeed, let's aim big and start with Socrates, political philosophy's supposed forefather. Here the big question is: What *difference*, if any, did he make to the world? Presumably *some* difference or he wouldn't have been put to death, in 399 BC, for 'impiety' and 'corrupting the young'. Presumably, if he had had *no* influence, it seems unlikely he would have been thought so dangerous. Yet maybe those who condemned Socrates *were* mistaken. After all, it's hard to pin down not just what difference he made to Athenian politics but even what difference he was *trying* to make, given that he himself never wrote anything down.

Let's look instead, then, at Plato, Socrates' pupil, as well as the pilot of his legacy. Presumably, to the extent that we have any idea of Socrates' views, we have them via the words put in his mouth in Plato's dialogues. Yet what difference did *he* make? Sure, philosophy in general was once famously described as 'footnotes to Plato', but what about his *political* legacy? Again, it's hard to pin down. Yes, we see his *intellectual* influences wherever we look, from Freud's tripartite model of the mind to Huxley's *Brave New World*, but how often do politicians reference him in their speeches, let alone actually try to *build* his *Republic*?

Maybe then we should already give up. Despite having only glanced at Socrates and Plato, perhaps it's already clear that the prudent thing to do here would be to quit while we're behind. Yet that wouldn't be the *philosophical* thing to do. The philosophical thing to do, instead, is to draw on our love of 'analysis', as discussed, and think more broadly about this concept of *influence* we've been invoking without scrutinising. After all, consider here that one can be influential not just by directly influencing politics but also by influencing someone else with political influence, or indeed someone who influences somebody else with influence, and so on and so forth. And, at the same time, we can also influence people not just in the sense that they adopt our point of view but also in the sense that they react against what we're telling them. This is often how parents influence their children, sadly enough, but also, wonderfully, how both philosophical and political argument tends to progress.

So, with this idea in mind, consider now a third famous figure from the ancient world – Cicero. This is someone who excelled not just at philosophical argument but also at political rhetoric. This is someone who, three hundred years after Plato, rose swiftly through Roman public life, first as a lawyer and renowned orator and then as the consul who saved his country from a coup, though in doing so, crucially, he put to death those conspirators without the benefit of a proper trial. This is someone who, shortly after that decision, and having finished his term as consul, was exiled from Rome, though he later returned and played a key part in the final days of his beloved republic as it was torn apart by the power struggle between Pompey and Caesar. This is someone who, despite all that political work, also found the time to write not just countless letters and speeches but also several books of lasting significance.[9]

We have here, in other words, a scholar and a statesman, a philosopher and a politician. Yet what exactly does his example tell us? Well, consider the following three points. First, one of those books just mentioned was entitled *On the Laws*, a counterpoint to Plato's final text of the same title, while the other, his real political masterpiece, and a text of which we still have only a quarter, with even that being lost for roughly 1,600 years, was entitled *On the Republic*, again with Plato's work in mind. Second, this latter text took the form of a dialogue, again following Plato. Third, this dialogue featured an inspirational protagonist, the politician Scipio, rather than the philosopher Socrates, again under Plato's influence. Surely, then, this is someone who not only held huge political influence but who was also influenced himself by earlier philosophy. Surely, although Cicero differed on various key points from Plato, praising the practical virtues of the Romans over the contemplative Greeks, and praising thoughtful politicians over those with solely philosophical experience, the influence of the earlier figure is undeniable, such that it is hard to imagine what he wrote being remotely similar without it. Surely, we have here proof of the influence of philosophy on politics.

# Why?

It might help to put it like this. Do we really think that Cicero's many renowned speeches, given in the Senate and elsewhere, and concerned as they were with fundamental questions of legitimacy, justice, and so on, had nothing to do with his philosophical reading of, and engagement with, Plato and his fellow Greeks?[10] Do we really think that the republican position Cicero took in these speeches had no relationship at all with the political decisions he made to the same effect? Do we *really* want to say that his thoughts, as expressed by his words, had nothing to do with his actions? Clearly, his ideas mattered, or he would hardly have shared them and risked his life for them. Clearly, if that's true, the influences on those thoughts also matter. Clearly, if all this holds true, political philosophy can change the world, given that it has done so at least once before.

The point to dwell on here is this: Cicero, as a political actor as well as a philosophical author, was both *drawing on* and *responding to* Plato. And not just Plato. In terms of the content of his argument, as opposed to its style, he actually responded even more to Aristotle, who *himself* responded to Plato and who was once, to boot, tutor and advisor to Alexander the Great. At the same time, he also drew on Polybius, who again drew on *both* Plato and Aristotle, bearing in mind that Polybius was, among other things, both a captured slave of and advisor to Cicero's Roman political hero, Scipio. Again, then: influence, influence, influence.

Consider also here that part of the point of Cicero's *On the Republic*, the final text we have of any kind from before the fall of the Roman Republic under Julius Caesar, is to celebrate Rome as it was in what he saw as its heyday, back in the days of Scipio. Focusing on an era that many of his contemporaries also admired, his aim was to try and draw out the ordered principles that gave Rome the success it had at that time, as expressed by its then constitution. He is then, all at once, responding to Plato and others, writing for philosophers and politicians, and trying to change the world around him by trying to influence the plans and motivations of the various key actors of his day. And, indeed, he even got to return to political life, at the end of his days, to try and defend his beloved constitution from the battle of the dictators that followed Caesar's death, a position for which he lost his life, with his tongue nailed to a wall as a symbol of the death of Roman Republican politics. And why does that symbolism matter? Because, again, it shows the power of ideas. We only symbolically kill ideas if ideas can make a difference, just as we only symbolically kill philosophers if philosophers can make a difference. As noted at the start of our story, if books never mattered, no one would ever burn them.

We might, however, think that this extended tale of Cicero is an exceptional one, focused on a rare example of what Plato would have called a 'philosopher king' and with little bearing on the normal run of things. As a result, we might ask now: Where exactly do these ideas go next? After all, if they are not seen in the Roman Empire that follows the republic, and if they are not seen in the Chinese or Islamic civilisations[11] that rise as the empire falls, where exactly do they go? Do they not just die? Were they not killed with Cicero? And, if so, was that then the end of the line for this thread of thought that ran from Plato to Aristotle to Polybius to Cicero, as well as from Plato to Cicero directly?

In one sense, yes, given that, as touched on already, the

written text of *On the Republic* was lost in its entirety between around 400 AD and 1825 AD, at which point it emerged in an Italian monastery, and even then with only a quarter of the manuscript available. Nevertheless, the core ideas of the text lived on, together with several of Cicero's other works, and one obvious answer to the question of 'where they went' would be to say that they re-emerged, with real force, on the same Italian peninsula on which they were written, around 1,500 years later. This re-emergence, famously, came with the rise of several dynamic and often republican city-states, including Venice, Genoa, and Florence, with the last of them being of particular interest, given that it is here that we see the emergence of yet another philosopher with political ambitions: Niccolò Machiavelli.

Again, this was someone writing for an audience that included powerful political actors, among them Lorenzo de' Medici, to whom *The Prince* is dedicated. Yet that was not Machiavelli's greatest work. Despite its fame, and despite the *realpolitik* for which it is generally known, it is in his *Discourses on Livy* that we see a renewed defence of republican government, as well as a renewal of the idea that political ideals might flow from philosophical wisdom rather than religious scripture. This, of course, is part of the more general *Renaissance* of classical ideas but also part of a returned sense that intellectual endeavour could, once more, be an important part of public political life – an idea that had long been squeezed to the margins by both monarchy and Christianity. Combining both an engagement with earlier scholars and a study of the political history of various city-states, including Rome above all others, this work gave new life to the Ciceronian ideal of blending philosophical reflection with political experience. It also gives us at least one answer to the question not just of whether Plato-via-Cicero had any further influence but also of what form that influence took.

There is, however, an even grander answer available. Building further on this legacy that runs from the ancients to the Renaissance, what we see three centuries later is the start of something beyond even Cicero's imagination, bearing in mind the size of the Roman territories in his lifetime.[12] This is the birth of the American republic, signalled first in 1776 with the Declaration of Independence, and then again in 1787 with the drafting of the federal constitution. The second of these documents is of particular interest, given that both the constitution itself and the public arguments made in its favour, published most famously in the *Federalist Papers*, testify not just to the appeal of the Roman Republic and everything that had been written about its guiding principles down the years but also, by extension, to Plato and Cicero's legacy. This is a constitution that would define a country the size of a continent, running from ocean to ocean, and it was bound together by ideals that spread from ancient Greece, to republican Rome, to Renaissance Europe, and now finally over the Atlantic. With each of those steps, of course, we see these ideas revisited and developed by new philosophical minds and political actors, but also something else. We see the broader move that interests us here – from arguments to actions and from philosophy to politics.

It's worth looking especially closely at this case of applied political philosophy in order to see all the ways in which it chimes with our story so far. Consider here, for example, that the authors of the *Federalist Papers* – Madison, Hamilton, and Jay – gave themselves the collective pen-name of *Publius*, a hero of the liberation of Rome from its kings. Consider that their chief critic called himself *Brutus*, yet another hero of that same liberation. Consider that, at Jefferson's bidding, the American seat of government sits on a piece of land renamed Capitol Hill, after the Capitoline hill on which the Roman Senate and Temple of Jupiter could be found. And, indeed, consider even that the names of so many towns in the north-eastern United States now have the names of city-states of the ancient Greco-Roman world, from Syracuse to Ithaca, though one stands out even above these: Tully, in New York, takes its name from a certain Marcus Tullius Cicero.

So, once more, Rome and Cicero *mattered*, at least in the long run, along with the Greeks that preceded them and the Renaissance Europeans that followed them. Ideas can fade away but also return with a vengeance. Political philosophy can drift into the background but also return at key moments, including when the groundwork for so much of our political future is being laid. Yes, it is often marginalised, condemned, and forgotten. Yes, it is not always present. But it is always potent. Today's American politicians may not know what their ancestors knew, yet they sit all the same at the head of a country whose political system is defined by two thousand years of philosophical argument. What more, then, could we want here? If shaping the character of the world's most powerful state doesn't count as influence, we might ask, then what does?

Perhaps then this journey, from Plato to Cicero, and from Rome to Washington, is encouragement enough in terms of the history of political ideas and the history of political practice, because it shows that at least one idea, or set of ideas, can change the world for millennia to come. Yet our story doesn't quite end there. Switching to the present, we might also take in Philip Pettit, one of several contemporary philosophers dedicating themselves to a broadly 'republican' way of answering political philosophy's organising question. This is an answer that focuses on a certain kind of liberty as 'non-domination' and which takes its lead from, *inter alia*, both Roman practice and Ciceronian argument. Pettit is important here, because it was with this work in mind, in 2002, that he was asked to put together republican policy proposals for the Spanish prime minister José Luis Rodríguez Zapatero and, later, to assess his achievements in light of them.[13] If, therefore, we want yet another illustration of political philosophy's potential, then here it is: a straightforward story involving just one philosopher, one ordering of principles, one politician, and one country.

Of course, in the normal run of things, influence is rarely as clear as this, given the diffuse and complex ways in which ideas spread and get put into practice, making Pettit and Zapatero, perhaps, the perfect final chapter to our story here. It also might transpire that no one runs again with these ideas for a thousand years. Yet, even if that is right, it would only remind us of the enduring power of ideas and the arguments around them. Consider, for example, that *Star Wars* takes its narrative from the fall of the Roman Republic, just as Aldous Huxley took his lead, in *Brave New World*, from Plato's *Republic*. In the former, notice, it is 'Senator Palpatine' who destroys the 'republic', having taken advantage of its wealth, scale, and corruption, before introducing an 'empire' under his own control, all while being looked after by 'Palatine' guards. We might, then, say something like this: if Renaissance Europe and Enlightenment America could take inspiration from the arguments of long-dead political philosophers, and if contemporary science fiction can do the same, then why not future utopian practice, despite whatever lull in political experimentation we see in the meanwhile? Just as we take so many of our ideals from a time long, long ago, eventually they might end up shaping a galaxy far, far away.

Perhaps, though, we should consider just a few more examples, in briefer terms, of the general move from philosophy to practice that interests us here. These take place at least one remove from the Plato-to-Pettit tale we've been telling so far and start instead with Jean-Jacques Rousseau, who interests us for at least four reasons. First, because he shares an ideal held by many though not all 'republicans': of small self-governing city-states. Second, because he shares with Plato an idea of freedom as self-rule, according to which the better, reasoning part of your mind is in charge of your base desires, as well as your petty obsessions with social status. Third, because, like Cicero, he was a leading intellectual of his time: a best-selling novelist and counter-Enlightenment philosopher who became a literary and intellectual star of Enlightenment Europe.[14] Fourth, and most importantly, because he was the author of *The Social Contract*, a text from which so many in the French Revolution took their inspiration, with so much of the rest of the world then taking their inspiration from that revolution. As a result, we have here, once again, someone who engaged with earlier political philosophers, who inspired later political actors, and whose words and arguments came to animate an event that inspired much of the world, as captured by Wordsworth in that famous line 'Bliss it was in that dawn to be alive, But to be young was very heaven!'

Rousseau's influence, though, runs even further than the French Revolution. Just as he influenced those directly involved with politics, he also influenced those who themselves went on to influence later politicians. Consider Karl Marx, for example, who takes much of his early inspiration from Rousseau, and in particular his *Discourse on the Origins of Inequality*, sharing not only his view of modern human 'nature' as the product of exploitative circumstances but also his view that we once enjoyed a simpler but more egalitarian life, in which, perfectly naturally, we cared rather less for petty possessions and social status. And how important was Marx? Well, we might plausibly say that, without Marx, no Marxism; without *The Communist Manifesto*, no communism; and, without communism, what would China, Russia, Cuba, or Eastern Europe be today? And what about *Western* Europe? Would European social democracy be as benevolent without the threat of communism? Would the UK's Beveridge Report have been adopted, and even begrudgingly accepted by the likes of Churchill, if not for the need to win an *ideological* battle with communist intellectuals at home and abroad? Yes, of course, precise and certain answers to these questions are impossible, but the fact that the world would be a very *different* place without this intellectual input is undeniable. Philosophers influenced Marx, and Marx, as he said we must, did not simply interpret the world – he changed it.[15]

So, from Plato, to Cicero, to the American

Constitution, to Zapatero's Spain, and from Plato, to Rousseau, to Marx, to the communist states of what used to be called the 'Second World' and, in turn, the 'First World' that responded to it. And these are just two tales, though admittedly rather grand ones. Lesser known tales, in recent times, include William Galston, a leading 'value-pluralist', working in the upper echelons of Bill Clinton's administration; Marc Stears, a contemporary 'political realist' and co-author of 'Blue Labour', working as Ed Miliband's chief speechwriter for three years, when Miliband was leader of the Labour Party, and thus of the official opposition in British politics; and Tariq Modood and Charles Taylor, 'multiculturalists' who have helped to shape the ethnic, racial, religious, and indeed national politics of Britain, Canada, and beyond. And so it goes on: philosophers shaping political events and in turn being shaped by those events – sometimes visibly and sometimes invisibly, sometimes fundamentally and sometimes trivially.

Let's pause here though and dwell on just one micro-case within this larger macro-trend. This is the recent notion of 'pre-distribution', one idea among several that were floating around at the time during which Stears, as just mentioned, moved from academic political philosophy to political practice. The idea is simple at heart. It says that, rather than just *re*distributing money via taxation, one could also *pre*distribute it differently by altering either the wages received in the first place or the costs borne by those who have already been taxed and paid. One might, for example, change the amount ordinary citizens pay in their energy bills, and it was for just such a proposal, as part of a broader speech, that Stears won *The Spectator*'s prize for political speech-making in 2014. This proposal was initially ridiculed by parts of both government and the media, but it was later adopted by the governing Conservative Party, only for them to drop it again following the 2017 general election campaign. And what happens next? Well, we don't know of course at this point. All we know is that a general idea, floated about in academic circles, made its way into politics via the work of someone who, like Cicero, was a philosopher with a knack for writing good speeches. Again, then, ideas and their authors matter – the ideas float in, they move around, they float out, they get whispered in ears, written on placards, and shouted from rooftops. Sometimes, of course, they get forgotten, but they never die altogether. From Cicero to communism, the authors and arguments are always 'out there', waiting to be put into action.

We might also frame this small example in yet another way. Let's say that what we are looking at here is an idea that goes, when fully understood, from James Meade, to John Rawls, to Jacob Hacker in a piece for Policy Exchange,[16] to a programme for government for a party currently out of power,[17] and then finally to the partial adoption of that programme by the government of the day – once they've disparaged it of course. Yet what's the most interesting thing about all of that? Perhaps the fact that the public don't even *see* it. What they'll see, if they notice it at all, is a suggestion for an energy price cap and then the criticism that idea receives from the other side. They certainly won't see that it was announced in a speech that won a prize or that this speech was written by a political philosopher. They'll just see the idea of the cap and a few claims on either side of it. And indeed, if told, they might just say, 'Well,

*I* could have thought of an energy price cap. It's hardly *genius* is it?'

There's all the difference, however, between an isolated policy, or a random assortment of policies, and a coherent set of them, as informed by a clear set of principles, both in terms of how effective an overall government programme is and in terms of how much electoral success it is likely to attract in the first place. Consider, for example, that in recent times the UK has seen two hugely significant political programmes, the first led by Margaret Thatcher in the 1980s and the second by Tony Blair in the 1990s and 2000s. These were, for better or worse, transformative episodes in British politics, and they were led and defined by fairly clear and coherently assembled ideas. Of course there are inconsistencies and compromises along the way, and of course the politicians spend a good deal of their time responding to events they never expected rather than putting into place the plans they had when they had the time to think about them. Yet the ideas and those arguments surrounding them still matter. *Clear* ideas about states and markets led to the privatisation of public housing and utilities in one decade and the rebuilding of hospitals and schools in another. *Clear* ideas about freedom, equality, and community are not just a part of how we explain the birth of such policies, historically speaking, but also how we explain their political success.

There is, though, still more to be said here about different cases and the logistics they illustrate. Sticking with the same British context a little longer, we might consider, for example, that, in 1965, Justice Devlin engaged in a much publicised debate with H. L. A. Hart about the possibility of decriminalising homosexuality. This was a wide-ranging and fundamental debate about the nature of law and the place of morality within it, and one key position taken by Hart, a leading political and legal philosopher, was as follows. He said that we should adopt an attractive and general principle according to which government should not interfere with an individual unless they are doing something that harms somebody else. From speech to sexuality, from drinking to smoking, and from production to consumption, this is a principle that gives us clear guidance, and it does so even though it stems from a text written back in 1862, and to which we have already turned earlier, in chapter 3 – Mill's *On Liberty*. Mill himself, as it happens, was also a leading intellectual of his day, who spoke out as an occasional democrat, a constant liberal, and a proto-feminist, and even worked as an MP for several years. Yet it was this one simple idea, revisited here by Hart, 103 years after the publication of the book that contained it, that gives him his greatest political influence. In Mill's case, therefore, we see not just that political work and philosophical enquiry can be *combined*, as they were with Cicero, but also that the latter can, in time, prove much more *politically* significant than the former.

The real lesson here, then, is not really about *Mill* at all, or even Hart, or even the fact that Hart's position eventually won the day, with homosexuality decriminalised in 1967. The lesson is that, in the long run, principles matter more than people, philosophy more than philosophers, and political ideas more than day-to-day politics. Though Mill, Hart, and Devlin are all dead, the idea that government should not interfere with us unless we are harming others lives on. Of course, this is not the *only* idea that guides us – we accept being taxed in order to help others, even when we are doing no harm to them – but we see it today in all sorts of spheres, from our laws regarding incitement and hate speech to the banning of drink-driving and public smoking. In each case, crucially, a new legal restriction came into place only when it was accepted that some or other group of people was being 'harmed' by something that had previously been regarded as a harmless and thus private choice. So, once more, what was once part of a book is now part of our lives.

What, then, happens next? Well, sticking purely to the British context, we might point out here that, as things currently stand, Jonathan Wolff, an egalitarian, sits on government commissions and engages in public life on issues ranging from drugs policy, to gambling, to train safety systems;[18] Onora O'Neill, a Kantian, sits in the House of Lords and works on, among other things, medical ethics, banking standards, and ongoing media reform;[19] while Bhikhu Parekh, a multiculturalist, sits again in the House of Lords, and again, like O'Neill, works on a range of issues as and when they fly on and off the agenda.[20] Perhaps, though, some will wonder here: exactly what difference have these three ever made? But that is the wrong question. Yes, they have made an important and tangible difference to our current political scene, yet that might be just the start of their influence. Right now, material interests, party loyalty, personal deals, compromises, mistakes, bullying, lobbying – all of these and more are muddying the waters. Their true legacy, and indeed the legacy of philosophers with no public profile at all, might not emerge for some time to come. This is what past experience tells us and what we should expect of our politico-philosophical future. We know that ideas matter, together with the authors who articulate them, but not *which* ideas will turn out to matter the most. We know that political philosophers matter, but not *which* ones will be known, just by their surname, in a thousand years' time. And that's as it should be. We should be glad, both that the past influence of political philosophy is clear and that its future course is uncertain. Among other things, it reminds us that part of the point of political philosophy is to shape the future, given that the future has yet to be decided and is still up for grabs, at least for those bold and clever enough to produce the ideas that matter.

## 4.6 Students and movements

I said a moment ago that even the kinds of connections just discussed sometimes happen without our noticing. This is true, but it's also true that even more intangible changes happen all the time without our noticing, and that these in turn are part of the point of political philosophy. This becomes clear once we think about the fact that, when political philosophers are not reading or writing, they are often teaching. Whom, then, are they teaching? Students, obviously. But what do those students then become? A few of them, naturally, become politicians. Bernard Crick, for example, once taught David Blunkett at Sheffield University, with Blunkett then asking Crick, decades later, to put together a citizenship curriculum for him during his tenure as education secretary, the content of which would influence generations to come.[21] Yet most of our teaching is less palpable in its political effects. Some of our students, for example, become teachers who teach pupils who become politicians. Some of them become people who advise politicians. Some of them become journalists who pressure and influence politicians and their voters. Some of them become business people who buy or bend the ear of politicians. Some of them become activists who pressure politicians through protests and campaigns. Some of them become civil servants who advise politicians. And all of them, at least in democracies, become voters – voters who talk to other voters and who spread ideas and arguments throughout the wider population.

In some contexts, this move from education to influence is particularly intense. Consider, for example, that a typical day in British politics might involve an argument between the prime minister, the leader of the opposition, several key cabinet figures, and various leading journalists. That much is familiar. What is less familiar is that these people, for better or worse, all often share the same undergraduate background – a degree in 'PPE' from Oxford,[22] in which political philosophy is a core element. As a result, we shouldn't just say that our subject is somehow 'out there' in the world. It would be more accurate to say that it's everywhere, including at the very top. Although we might assume that it is somehow a 'big deal' within the ivory tower yet of only minor interest outside it, the reverse is closer to the truth. Within universities, it is one of a thousand subjects, whereas within politics it runs through everything we see, even when those carrying it out have no idea that that is what they are doing. On this point, it is worth quoting Keynes at length:

> The ideas of economists and political philosophers, both when they are right and when they are wrong, are more powerful than is commonly understood. Indeed the world is

ruled by little else. Practical men, who believe themselves to be quite exempt from any intellectual influence, are usually the slaves of some defunct economist. Madmen in authority, who hear voices in the air, are distilling their frenzy from some academic scribbler of a few years back. I am sure that the power of vested interests is vastly exaggerated compared with the gradual encroachment of ideas. Not, indeed, immediately, but after a certain interval; for in the field of economic and political philosophy there are not many who are influenced by new theories after they are twenty-five or thirty years of age, so that the ideas which civil servants and politicians and even agitators apply to current events are not likely to be the newest. But, soon or late, it is ideas, not vested interests, which are dangerous for good or evil.[23]

We should, though, be slightly more cautious than Keynes is here, and especially so given that stories involving Oxford 'PPE' and British politics, let alone stories such as that of Crick and Blunkett, are far from universal. We also do not want to start saying that, *whenever* and *however* political philosophy is present, it is somehow also potent, persuasive, and powerful. For example, we can find business leaders with an education in philosophy, and even some who claim it made a real difference to them,[24] but should not presume, without investigating, that they would have behaved differently with a different background.[25] We can find philosophers who debate the nature and purpose of their subject 'in public',[26] and even some who offer concrete guidance on topical issues,[27] but should not presume that anyone with power is listening. We even sometimes find 'celebrity' philosophers, such as Herbert Marcuse, who once refused an interview to *Playboy* unless he too got to pose nude in its pages,[28] but should not presume that such a simple statement was beyond other luminary figures, including those with more fame but less education.

And, indeed, even when we do find politicians with philosophical leanings, we should tread carefully. President Xi Jinping, for example, is currently having his 'political philosophy' written into the Chinese Constitution,[29] yet, given his background, is that really an *engagement* with the subject, in any meaningful sense, or just a function of power and political experience? Perhaps it is just an ideology with pretensions, bearing in mind here that, even when we do track down individuals with a clear background in politics or philosophy,[30] and even when those individuals have PhDs,[31] they often line up on different sides of key political issues. As a result, we might wonder, has all this education made them wiser or just more sophisticated? Consider here, for example, the awkward case of Saif al-Islam Gaddafi, who gained his PhD from the LSE in 2008.[32] Sure, this ended up affecting the LSE, but did it make any difference to Libya? If his story proves anything when it comes to political philosophy, it is only this: mere presence is no proof of influence, just as influence is no proof of improvement. Aristotle was Alexander the Great's tutor, not his advisor, and unfortunately our subject will sometimes be just a dash of sophistry here and a sprinkle of legitimacy there, at which point we'll be yearning for the irrelevance we had thought to avoid.

The key point here, however, is not that the connections just described cannot be made at all – we do not want to push too much that way. It is simply that we ought to look carefully before drawing conclusions. Political philosophy should not flatter itself and presume, *just* from these facts, that it has been a vital or valuable influence in every instance.

There is though a more exciting possibility buried among all these cases. Instead of just combining philosophical enquiry with political elitism – an enlightened leader here, a sophisticated parliament there – perhaps we should think now about reaching thousands, millions, even billions of people. Bearing in mind this role of philosopher as teacher, and adding that up, philosopher by philosopher, there's the potential here to influence not just a few democratic politicians but also the very *demos* those politicians hope to convince. Or, put differently, political philosophers have it in them to change *the people* in the sense of changing their *ideas* and, in turn, what they take to be their *interests*, which politicians, naturally enough, try to convince them they represent.

Think here, by analogy, of how much better politics works in literate versus illiterate societies, and of how much better it operates in ones in which people finish school at eighteen rather than eight. What then of a population educated, to some degree or other, in political philosophy? Returning to an idea first floated at the start of this book, we can begin to imagine here just how much better politics might proceed if everyone had a basic level of competence in this subject.[33] No more falling for vague or inconsistent ideas. No more limiting of the imagination to just two or three principles or two or three ways of ordering them. No more following politicians who offered only platforms expressing such things. Or at least: *less* of all those things. The great hope here, however, is this: a different *demos* might get you a different *democracy* and, in turn, a different *politics*.

This move, from the practice of political philosophy

to its potential, is a significant one for the 'point' of our subject. It implies that our civic role is not just about arguing with each other and then hoping one day for a phone call from an old university friend, or about the chance to play special advisor to someone who already matters, or even about educating, in the corridors of the world's great universities, tomorrow's political elite. It's also about educating on a grand scale. And, note: *educating*, not *indoctrinating*. The idea here is certainly not that philosophers could or should be turning students into junior republicans, Kantians, or Rawlsians. It's rather that the grasp of a whole range of ideas, and the skill to handle them, could be rolled out as surely as one rolls out numeracy, literacy, or even the new educational holy grail, 'coding'. Imagine, for example, that we rolled out a certain kind of 'philosophical coding' across 'secondary' or 'high' schools in countries around the world, or even just across more university courses for now. All that would mean is expanding what we already do in existing university courses – guiding analysis, encouraging critique, and discussing possible orderings of principles, all while letting students argue and decide for themselves. In doing so, surely, we would be producing better students but also, in time, better voters, and even better politicians, once they are held to account by this new breed of people they represent.

So, all we need to do here is imagine a world in which political philosophy had, not just the significant influence it already has, as argued for already, but also a role beyond that. Or, from a different angle, perhaps we should just imagine a world without *any* political philosophy at all. With this thought we return to our earlier discussion regarding the societal benefits of the subject, and again we ask: What exactly *would* such a world be like? Surely it would be something like this: no clarity regarding our key concepts; no careful critique of the different values or principles available to us; no expansion of that list of values and principles via new innovations; and no sustained attempts to order them in ways that we might want to adopt as policy platforms. In such a world, we can be confident, there would be less chance of anything like 'the truth' emerging or of 'progress' occurring, because we would never undertake sustained thinking about even those ideas tried out so far, let alone those which might be tried in the future. George Santayana once remarked that those who forget history are doomed to repeat it. Well, societies that don't do political philosophy *at all* would be doomed to repeat their politics, *ad infinitum*. So long as there is no serious thinking about the mistakes of the past and possibilities of the future; so long as there is no serious thinking about the principles at the roots of those possibilities and mistakes and about how they might be ordered – what chance is there of us having a better world, or even figuring out what one would look like?

Perhaps, though, if that still doesn't quite persuade you, it's worth considering just one last point. Consider here, if only briefly, what happens when political philosophers exit stage left. Obviously enough, some other set of smooth talkers enter stage right. Gurus, columnists, or academic experts of some other variety – scientists with political opinions, economists with political certainty, lawyers wanting to put into statute, for ever after, things that they wouldn't trust to the unwashed masses. Or perhaps another set of people altogether. Perhaps, the more the vacuum grows where political philosophy should operate, the more scope there is for vested interests to trump good ideas.

With this in mind, we might look back to the 'neoliberal' politics of Margaret Thatcher and Ronald Reagan during the 1980s, a time when we see not just the influence of philosopher-economists such as Friedrich von Hayek but also the influence of those they encouraged outside of politics, such as Antony Fisher. Fisher was someone who became the most successful chicken farmer in Europe following the adoption of battery farming methods that were way 'ahead' of his time, but also someone who didn't want simply to use the proceeds in order to *talk* to politicians. Instead, on Hayek's advice, he used them to found something once described as the 'most influential think tank in modern British history':[34] the Institute for Economic Affairs (IEA). The purpose of this entity, above all else, was to fight socialism and the welfare state while promoting 'markets' wherever possible. And there are parallels elsewhere. In Reagan's America, for example, we see the influence not just of thinkers such as Hayek, Milton Friedman, and so on, but also the billionaire Charles Koch, in this case through the funding of James Buchanan's work at George Mason University and through his funding of the influential Cato Institute. The project there, once again, was not just about reaching just one or two key people. It was about generating a whole network of similarly minded people, all of whom were either producing papers, or writing speeches, or making political decisions that changed the overall political tone.[35]

What, then, do these last examples tell us? They tell us, once more, that ideas matter, but also that the way they end up mattering isn't always down to their merits,

at least in the short run. It can be down to sponsor-
ship, and even censorship, whether from left or right,
and whether by corporations, individuals, or unions.
They also tell us that, if political philosophy is *not* an
integral part of society, with ideas and philosophers put
into competition with one another in front of enlightened voters and representatives, then maybe just a few
such philosophers will hold the ears that matter – and
maybe for reasons which, again, have less to do with
the strength of their cases and more to do with cases
of cash. All of which leaves us with two key problems.
First, a philosophically uneducated public is a public
that is more easily duped, bought, or misled. Second,
a public under the influence of just a few key thinkers,
of either left or right, is a public under which influence
is more easily bought. After all, as philosophers, we
are none of us rich, and it's easier to buy and boost the
careers of just a few scholars than it would be to buy the
entire profession. Taken together, these two problems
tell us something important about the idea of politico-
philosophical education: the first because it makes it a
form of inoculation; and the second because it makes
it a way of pricing vested interests out of the market –
though admittedly some of them won't mind that, given
how much they love markets.

## 4.7 Conclusions

We come now to the very end of the book. Part of *the*
point of political philosophy, I have argued here, is to
change the world, a process that can take many forms.
Part of *my* point has been to say that the world would
be a better place if we did even more of it and spread

it even more widely. Clearly, political philosophy has already changed the world and will continue to do so, whatever I say about it. Less clearly, what kind of political philosophy gets out there, and how much influence it has, are things that are up to us – first in the sense that we can argue about this as scholars and students, and second in the sense that we can then reach others with those arguments about how far political philosophy ought to be spread.

# Notes

## Chapter 1 Introduction

1 E. Rossi and M. Sleat, 'Realism in normative political theory', *Philosophy Compass* 9/10 (2014): 689–701.

2 L. Valentini, 'Ideal vs. non-ideal theory: a conceptual map', *Philosophy Compass* 7/9 (2012): 654–64.

3 A. Sen, *The Idea of Justice* (Cambridge, MA: Harvard University Press, 2011).

4 J. Waldron, 'Political political theory: an inaugural lecture', *Journal of Political Philosophy* 21/1 (2013): 1–23.

5 See, for example, those working on the analytic/continental split in political philosophy: C. Chin and L. Thomassen, 'Introduction: analytic, continental and the question of a bridge', *European Journal of Political Theory* 15/2 (2016): 133–7; but also J. Floyd, 'Analytics and continentals: divided by

nature but united by praxis?', *European Journal of Political Theory* 15/2 (2016): 155–71.

6 See 'The hedgehog and the fox', in I. Berlin, *The Proper Study of Mankind* (London: Chatto & Windus, 1997), pp. 436–98. See also, more recently, R. Dworkin, *Justice for Hedgehogs* (Cambridge, MA: Harvard University Press, 2011).

7 J. Floyd, 'Is political philosophy too ahistorical?', *Critical Review of International Social and Political Philosophy* 12/4 (2009): 513–33; J. Floyd, 'Historical facts and political principles: a reply to De Angelis', *Critical Review of International Social and Political Philosophy* 14/1 (2011), 89–90; J. Floyd, 'From historical contextualism, to mentalism, to behaviourism', in J. Floyd and M. Stears (eds), *Political Philosophy versus History?* (Cambridge: Cambridge University Press, 2011), pp. 38–64; J. Floyd, 'Relative value and assorted historical lessons', ibid., pp. 206–25; J. Floyd, 'Why the history of ideas needs more than just ideas', *Intellectual History Review* 21/1 (2011): 27–42.

8 J. Floyd, 'Should political philosophy be more realistic?', *Res Publica* 16/3 (2010): 337–47. But also, more recently, J. Floyd, 'Should global political theory get real?', *Journal of International Political Theory* 12/2 (2016): 93–5; J. Floyd, 'Normative behaviourism and global political principles', *Journal of International Political Theory* 12/2 (2016): 152–68; and J. Floyd, 'Normative behaviourism as a solution to four problems in realism and non-ideal theory', *Critical Review of International Social and Political Philosophy* 21 (2018), https://doi.org/10.1080/1369 8230.2018.1501538.

9  J. Floyd, 'Raz on practical reason and political moral-
   ity', *Jurisprudence* 8/2 (2017): 185–204; J. Floyd,
   'Rawls' methodological blueprint', *European
   Journal of Political Theory* 16/3 (2017): 367–81.

10 J. Floyd, *Is Political Philosophy Impossible?
   Thoughts and Behaviour in Normative Political
   Theory* (Cambridge: Cambridge University Press,
   2017). If you're wondering about my answer to
   the titular question, it's roughly that: no, I don't
   think political philosophy is impossible, but yes, it is
   very hard, at least for me. More seriously, the core
   argument is that political philosophers should do a
   bit less thinking about our thoughts (our intuitions,
   considered judgements, and so on) and a bit more
   thinking about our behaviour (When do we rebel?
   When do we turn to crime?) when it comes to the
   task of justifying political principles.

11 See    www.ipsos.com/ipsos-mori/en-uk/politicians-
   are-still-trusted-less-estate-agents-journalists-and-
   bankers.

12 This is not to say they lack expertise in anything
   – I am not at all anti-politicians. It's just that it's
   unclear what expertise their job requires, whether
   they have it, and how one would get such a thing.

## Chapter 2 What?

1 Sometimes called departments of 'government'
  or 'political science', though look out also for
  departments of 'international relations', 'political
  economy', and even 'war studies', as political philosophers can be found lurking in all of them. Note
  also that some of our best political philosophers are
  found in law departments, from Kimberley Brownlee

to Martha Nussbaum, and in history departments, including most notably Quentin Skinner. For my part, I'm in a 'School' of Sociology, Politics, and International Relations.

2 Consider here that one of our leading journals, *Political Theory*, describes itself as an 'international journal of political philosophy'.

3 L. Strauss, *What is Political Philosophy? And Other Studies* (Chicago: University of Chicago Press, 1988), p. 12. Note that in a separate essay he used 'just' instead of 'good'. See L. Strauss, 'Political philosophy and history', *Journal of the History of Ideas* 10/1 (1949): 30.

4 T. M. Scanlon, *The Difficulty of Tolerance* (Cambridge: Cambridge University Press, 2003), p. 1. He also remarked, in an interview given to Harry Kreisler in 2007, that 'It has to do with our relations with each other that are mediated through the institutions we share.' The transcript of that interview is at http://globetrotter.berkeley.edu/people7/Scanlon/scanlon-cono.html.

5 M. Matravers, 'Twentieth-century political philosophy', in D. Moran (ed.), *The Routledge Companion to Twentieth Century Philosophy* (London: Routledge), p. 901.

6 N. McAfee, 'Feminist political philosophy', in the *Stanford Encyclopedia of Philosophy*, at http://plato.stanford.edu/entries/feminism-political/.

7 J. Rawls, *A Theory of Justice* (Cambridge, MA: Harvard University Press, 1971), p. 3.

8 I. Berlin, 'The pursuit of the ideal', in *The Proper Study of Mankind* (New York: Farrar, Straus, & Giroux, 1998), p. 1. Berlin uses this phrase again in

R. Jahanbegloo, *Conversations with Isaiah Berlin* (London: Prentice Hall, 1992).

9 I. Berlin, *Political Ideas in the Romantic Age: Their Rise and Influence on Modern Thought* (London: Chatto & Windus, 2006), p. 12.

10 S. Blackburn, *The Oxford Dictionary of Philosophy* (Oxford: Oxford University Press, 2005), p. 282.

11 M. Bevir (ed.), *Encyclopedia of Political Theory* (London: Sage, 2010), p. xxxiii.

12 B. Williams, *In the Beginning was the Deed: Realism and Moralism in Political Argument* (Princeton, NJ: Princeton University Press, 2005), p. 77.

13 B. Goodwin, *Using Political Ideas* (Chichester: Wiley, 2014), p. 4.

14 A. Swift, *Political Philosophy: A Beginners' Guide for Students and Politicians* (Cambridge: Polity, 2014), p. 5.

15 R. Nozick, *Anarchy, State, and Utopia* (New York: Basic Books, 1974), p. 4. See also his comments two pages later on the limits placed on political philosophy by *moral* philosophy. I say more about that relationship later in this chapter.

16 J. Plamenatz, 'The use of political theory', *Political Studies* 8 (1960): 37.

17 D. Miller, *Political Philosophy: A Very Short Introduction* (Oxford: Oxford University Press), p. 2.

18 P. Pettit, *Contemporary Political Theory* (London: Prentice Hall, 1991), p. 1.

19 J. Wolff, *An Introduction to Political Philosophy* (Oxford: Oxford University Press, 2006).

20 G. A. Cohen, *On the Currency of Egalitarian Justice, and Other Essays in Political Philosophy* (Princeton, NJ: Princeton University Press, 2011), p. 228.

21 J. Waldron, '*Political* political theory: an inaugural lecture', *Journal of Political Philosophy* 21/1 (2013): 1–23.

22 J. Rawls, *Justice as Fairness: A Restatement* (Cambridge, MA: Harvard University Press, 2001), pp. 1–4.

23 P. Pettit, *Republicanism: A Theory of Freedom and Government* (Oxford: Oxford University Press, 1997), pp. 2–3.

24 M. Walzer, *Spheres of Justice: A Defense of Pluralism and Equality* (New York: Basic Books, 1983), p. xiv.

25 A. James, 'Constructing justice for existing practice: Rawls and the status quo', *Philosophy and Public Affairs* 33 (2005): 281–316; and A. James, *Fairness in Practice: A Social Contract for a Global Economy* (Oxford: Oxford University Press, 2012), esp. pp. 25–31. See also A. Sangiovanni, 'Global justice, reciprocity, and the state', *Philosophy and Public Affairs* 35 (2007): 3–39.

26 R. Dworkin, *Justice for Hedgehogs* (London: Harvard University Press, 2011). For discussion of this value-holism, see R. S. Hansen, 'In defence of conceptual integration', *Res Publica* 23 (2017): 349–65.

27 K. A. Appiah and D. Kodsi, 'Interview with Kwame Anthony Appiah', *Oxford Review of Books*, http://the-orb.org/2017/09/20/interview-with-kwame-anthony-appiah/.

28 S. Wolin, *Politics and Vision: Political Philosophy from the Classic Problems of the Greeks to the Contemporary Problems of the 'Organization Man'* (London: Allen & Unwin, 1960), pp. 1–27. Note

that, although Wolin picks out several patterns and recurring themes within what he calls a 'tradition of discourse', and even at one point something that could function as an extremely vague definition – 'reflection on matters that concern the community as a whole' – the key point remains that he both (1) defines the subject as the sum of what people have contributed under its remit and (2) lacks a precise idea of that remit.

29 D. Held, *Political Theory Today* (Cambridge: Polity, 1991).

30 D. Knowles, *Political Philosophy* (London: Routledge, 2001), esp. pp. 2–3.

31 W. Kymlicka, *Contemporary Political Philosophy: An Introduction* (Oxford: Oxford University Press, 2002).

32 S. K. White and J. D. Moon, *What is Political Theory?* (London: Sage, 2004).

33 D. Leopold and M. Stears, *Political Theory: Methods and Approaches* (Oxford: Oxford University Press, 2008).

34 J. G. Gunnell, *The Descent of Political Theory: The Genealogy of an American Vocation* (London: University of Chicago Press, 1993); and A. Vincent, *The Nature of Political Theory* (Oxford: Oxford University Press, 2004).

35 A. Quinton, *Political Philosophy* (Oxford: Oxford University Press, 1967), pp. 1–18.

36 A. Blau (ed.), *Analytical Political Theory* (Cambridge: Cambridge University Press, 2017), pp. 6–7; and D. Miller and R. Dagger, 'Utilitarianism and beyond: contemporary analytical political theory', in T. Ball and R. Bellamy (eds), *The Cambridge History of*

*Twentieth-Century Political Thought* (Cambridge: Cambridge University Press, 2003), pp. 446–9.

37 S. Lukes, *Power: A Radical View* (Basingstoke: Palgrave Macmillan, 2004).

38 F. Nietzsche, *On the Genealogy of Morality* (Cambridge: Cambridge University Press, 2011), p. 53.

39 E. Rossi, 'Justice, legitimacy and (normative) authority for political realists', *Critical Review of International Social and Political Philosophy* 15/2 (2012): 149–64; F. Wendt, 'On realist legitimacy', *Social Philosophy and Policy* 32/2 (2016): 227–45.

40 G. Brock, *Global Justice: A Cosmopolitan Account* (Oxford: Oxford University Press, 2009); S. Caney, *Justice Beyond Borders: A Global Political Theory* (Oxford: Oxford University Press, 2006).

41 For a discussion of non-Western contributions to political thought which I think fit within my proposed definition here, see B. Parekh, 'Non-Western political thought', in *The Cambridge History of Twentieth-Century Political Thought*, pp. 553–78.

42 B. Barry, *Justice as Impartiality* (Oxford: Oxford University Press, 1995), p. 77.

43 A. Gibbard, *Reconciling our Aims: In Search of Bases for Ethics* (Oxford: Oxford University Press, 2008), p. 30. James Rachels follows a similar route for moral philosophy in the popular teaching text *The Elements of Moral Philosophy* (New York: McGraw-Hill, 2010), p. 1.

44 Gibbard, *Reconciling our Aims*, p. 59.

45 Miller and Dagger, 'Utilitarianism and beyond', p. 446.

46 Ibid., p. 448.

**Chapter 3 How?**

1 For survey works that organise their material around 'approaches' and/or 'methods', see D. Leopold and M. Stears (eds), *Political Theory: Methods and Approaches* (Oxford: Oxford University Press, 2008); and A. Blau (ed.), *Methods in Analytical Political Theory* (Cambridge: Cambridge University Press, 2017).

2 See, e.g., S. Lukes, *Power: A Radical View* (Basingstoke: Palgrave Macmillan, 2004); I. Berlin, *Four Essays on Liberty* (Oxford: Oxford University Press, 1969); D. Parfit, 'Equality and priority', *Ratio* 10/3 (1997): 202–21.

3 For the former, see Nozick's critique of Rawls in R. Nozick, *Anarchy, State, and Utopia* (New York: Basic Books, 1974). For the latter, see Cohen's critique of Nozick in G. A. Cohen, *Self-Ownership, Freedom, and Equality* (Cambridge: Cambridge University Press, 1995).

4 We might, for example, think that an abstract theory of legitimacy, based on the general notion of consent, is the most guidance political philosophy can offer the world, or we might think it can produce a detailed vision of democracy, together with a new global democratic model for today's globalised world. For contrasting views, with contrasting levels of detail, compare the latest realist and cosmopolitan offerings. For the former, see M. Sleat, 'Legitimacy in realist thought: between moralism and *realpolitik*', *Political Theory* 42/3 (2014): 314–37. For the latter, see G. Brock, *Global Justice: A Cosmopolitan Account* (Oxford: Oxford University Press, 2009).

5 I use 'feelings' in an open-ended sense here – inclusive of sentiments, judgements, intuitions, and so on. It is meant to reflect how an ordinary person might start off reflecting on and talking about their own normative thinking; it is not meant to signal an implicit commitment to non-cognitivism, with 'feelings' somehow trumping 'beliefs' or 'judgements'.

6 For one of many good examples of this kind of work, though one that distinguishes between 'opportunity' and 'outcome', see A. Phillips, 'Defending equality of outcome', *Journal of Political Philosophy* 12/1 (2004): 1–19.

7 J. Rawls, *A Theory of Justice* (Cambridge, MA: Harvard University Press, 1971), p. 73. Note that Rawls's own distinction in *Theory* was between 'fair equality of opportunity' and 'careers open to talents' – see pp. 73 ff.

8 See, e.g., D. Parfit, 'Equality and priority'. For clarity on the distinction between priority and sufficiency as guiding ideals, see A. Mason, *Levelling the Playing Field: The Idea of Equal Opportunity and its Place in Egalitarian Thought* (Oxford: Oxford University Press, 2006).

9 For two different ways of focusing on problems rather than ideals, see J. N. Shklar, *The Faces of Injustice* (New Haven, CT: Yale University Press, 1990), and A. Sen, *The Idea of Justice* (Cambridge, MA: Harvard University Press, 2011). It's also notable that Cohen, who otherwise wants to assert the *priority* of principles, does concede that we can *discover* them through *experiences*, which might include experiences of, say, injustice, inequality, confinement, exploitation, and so on. See

G. A. Cohen, *Rescuing Justice and Equality* (Cambridge, MA: Harvard University Press, 2009).

10 The full quote, from Alfred North Whitehead, runs: 'The safest general characterization of the European philosophical tradition is that it consists of a series of footnotes to Plato.' See A. N. Whitehead, *Process and Reality: An Essay in Cosmology* (London: Macmillan, 1979), p. 39.

11 Q. Skinner, *Liberty before Liberalism* (Cambridge: Cambridge University Press, 2012). In a text written after the lecture on which *Liberty before Liberalism* is based, Skinner concedes that most people now use the term 'republican' rather than 'neo-Roman'. See Q. Skinner, *Hobbes and Republican Liberty* (Cambridge: Cambridge University Press, 2008).

12 P. Pettit, *Republicanism: A Theory of Freedom and Government* (Oxford: Oxford University Press, 1997).

13 J.-J. Rousseau, *The Social Contract* (London: Penguin, 2012), ch. 8. See also B. Constant, *Political Writings* (Cambridge: Cambridge University Press, 1988).

14 For extended treatment of the analytic/continental split, see J. Floyd, 'Analytics and continentals: divided by nature but united by praxis?', *European Journal of Political Theory* 15/2 (2016): 155–71.

15 B. Barry, *Political Argument* (Berkeley: University of California Press, 1965).

16 D. Lyons, *Forms and Limits of Utilitarianism* (Oxford: Oxford University Press, 1965).

17 B. A. O. Williams, 'The idea of equality', in P. Laslett and W. G. Runciman (eds), *Philosophy, Politics and Society* (Oxford: Blackwell, 1962).

18 W. B. Gallie, 'Essentially contested concepts', *Proceedings of the Aristotelian Society* 56 (1955).

19 Berlin, *Four Essays on Liberty*.

20 And notice, on the topic of innovation, that a key precursor to Berlin's work was, in turn, Constant's distinction between the liberties of the 'Ancients' and 'Moderns'. See Constant, *Political Writings*.

21 This is clearest in Q. Skinner, 'A third concept of liberty', *Proceedings of the British Academy* 117 (2002): 237–68.

22 J. Rawls, *A Theory of Justice* (Cambridge, MA: Harvard University Press, 1971).

23 Ibid., pp. 34, 37, 259, 326, 331.

24 Ibid., pp. 23, 374.

25 Ibid., pp. 73, 150, 337, 480, 511.

26 Ibid., pp. 202, 230.

27 T. Hobbes, *Leviathan* (Cambridge: Cambridge University Press, 1996), p. 92.

28 Ibid., p. 109 (emphasis added).

29 Raz, however, does think some values and/or principles can be prioritised and that pluralism doesn't go all the way down, as it were. See, e.g., J. Raz, *The Morality of Freedom* (Oxford: Oxford University Press, 1986), p. 194.

30 Berlin, *Four Essays on Liberty*.

31 Hobbes, *Leviathan*, p. 150.

32 Ibid., p. 117.

33 Ibid., p. 88.

34 E. Burke, *Reflections on the Revolution in France* (Cambridge: Cambridge University Press, 2014), p. 79.

35 B. Williams, *In the Beginning was the Deed: Realism and Moralism in Political Argument* (Princeton,

NJ: Princeton University Press, 2005); but also R. Guess, *Philosophy and Real Politics* (Princeton, NJ: Princeton University Press, 2008).

36 S. Hampshire, *Justice is Conflict* (Princeton, NJ: Princeton University Press, 2001).

37 C. Taylor, 'What's wrong with negative liberty', in A. Ryan (ed.), *The Idea of Freedom: Essays in Honour of Isaiah Berlin* (Oxford: Oxford University Press, 1979).

38 Ibid.

39 See Berlin's essay on 'John Stuart Mill and the ends of life', in I. Berlin, *Four Essays on Liberty*.

40 J. S. Mill, *On Liberty* (London: Penguin, 2003). Mill claims that each individual has different needs and wants (p. 123); that each individual is the best judge of their own needs and wants (p. 77); that interference in another person's life is likely to be mistaken (p. 151); and that liberty strengthens the mind and steels us when looking into the 'abyss' (pp. 98, 122).

41 For discussion of prostitution and Mill, see J. Waldron, 'Mill on liberty and the Contagious Diseases Acts', in N. Urbinati and A. Zakaras (eds), *J. S. Mill's Political Thought: A Bicentennial Reassessment* (Cambridge: Cambridge University Press, 2007), pp. 11–42.

42 Opium was an issue about which Mill was clear in *On Liberty* (ch. 5).

43 The thalidomide scandal was the event that led to new legislation around the world designed to ensure the proper testing of medicines before they are permitted for use. Examples of this legislation include the Medicines Act in the UK (1968), Directive 65/65/

EEC1 in the EEC (1965), and the Kefauver Harris Amendment in the USA (1962).

44 The purity and safety of bread had been a long-standing problem at this point. See, e.g., P. B. Hutt and P. B. Hutt II, 'A history of government regulation of adulteration and misbranding of food', *Food Drug Cosmetic Law Journal* 39 (1984): 2–73.

45 K. Marx and F. Engels, 'The Communist Manifesto', in D. McLellan (ed.), *Karl Marx: Selected Writings* (Oxford: Oxford University Press, 1997), p. 192.

46 See 'On the Jewish Question', ibid., p. 63.

47 J.-J. Rousseau, *A Discourse on Inequality* (London: Penguin, 1984), ch. 1.

48 D. Diderot, *Diderot: Political Writings* (Cambridge: Cambridge University Press, 1992), p. 27.

49 As Charles Taylor once wrote: 'in order to understand properly what we are about, we have to understand how we got where we are.' See C. Taylor, 'Philosophy and its history', in R. Rorty, J. B. Schneewind and Q. Skinner (eds), *Philosophy in History* (Cambridge: Cambridge University Press, 1984), p. 28.

50 F. Nietzsche, *On the Genealogy of Morality* (Cambridge: Cambridge University Press, 2001).

51 Ibid., p. 17.

52 Ibid., p. 33.

53 Ibid., pp. 32–3.

54 See, e.g., P. Singer, 'Ethics and intuitions', *Journal of Ethics* 9/3 (2005): 331–52; P. Singer, *The Expanding Circle: Ethics, Evolution, and Moral Progress* (Princeton, NJ: Princeton University Press, 2011); and K. de Lazari-Radek and P. Singer, 'The objectivity of ethics and the unity of practical reason', *Ethics* 123/1 (2012): 9–31.

55 J. Floyd, *Is Political Philosophy Impossible? Thoughts and Behaviour in Normative Political Theory* (Cambridge: Cambridge University Press, 2017), ch. 1.

56 J. Floyd, 'Relative value and assorted historical lessons', in J. Floyd and M. Stears (eds), *Political Philosophy versus History? Contextualism and Real Politics in Contemporary Political Thought* (Cambridge: Cambridge University Press, 2011), pp. 206–25.

57 Floyd, *Is Political Philosophy Impossible?*

58 For a more complicated way of breaking down this process, see ibid., ch. 2.

59 This definition of 'normative thoughts' is found ibid.

60 P. Singer, 'Famine, affluence, and morality', *Philosophy and Public Affairs* 1/3 (1972): 229–43.

61 For an excellent and recent discussion of 'thought experiments' and 'intuition pumps' in political philosophy, see chapter 9 of K. Dowding, *The Philosophy and Methods of Political Science* (London: Palgrave, 2016), pp. 213–42. I came to Dowding's work too late to make much use of it in this book, so it is worth noting that his chapter on political philosophy is also a very useful source on, *inter alia*, conceptual analysis (pp. 225–8) and issues arising from the uses we (try to) make of the history of political thought (pp. 216–23).

62 For thoughts on the distinctiveness of mentalism from the natural sciences, see again Floyd, *Is Political Philosophy Impossible?*

63 Mill, *On Liberty*, p. 98.

64 H. L. A. Hart, 'Rawls on liberty and its priority',

*University of Chicago Law Review* 40/3 (1973): 554.

65 P. Van Parijs, 'Difference principles', in S. Freeman (ed.), *The Cambridge Companion to Rawls* (Cambridge: Cambridge University Press, 2003), pp. 200–40.

66 Plato, *Republic* (London: Penguin, 2005), p. 473.

67 J. Rawls, *Justice as Fairness: A Restatement* (Cambridge, MA: Harvard University Press, 2001), pp. 30–1. Rawls follows Daniels on this, who himself developed the distinction in discussion of Rawls's *Theory of Justice*. See N. Daniels, 'Wide reflective equilibrium and theory acceptance in ethics', *Journal of Philosophy* 76/5 (1979): 256–82.

68 Rawls also invokes 'full reflective equilibrium' as a state of affairs whereby a society has achieved both general reflective equilibrium and also, and presumably in part for that reason, certain other features of what he calls a 'well-ordered society'. See ibid., p. 61.

69 So, the real appeal of reflective equilibrium as a method, in any of its guises, ultimately comes down to whether it expresses principles to which we already adhere, even if we only discover such principles via the application of reflective equilibrium. We might, for example, realise that this method expresses better than any other method a principle such as 'make your normative thoughts as systematic as possible' or 'consider all candidate political principles, together with their implications for various problems and values, before adopting any one set of them.' We do, though, have to hold that principle in order to get it started, or, if we are happy to experiment with it anyway, we at least

have to hold that principle for the results of the
process to have some kind of force for us.

70 See, e.g., C. Larmore, *The Morals of Modernity*
(Cambridge: Cambridge University Press, 1996).

71 This is what MacIntyre does in A. MacIntyre,
*Whose Justice? Which Rationality?* (Notre Dame,
IN: University of Notre Dame Press, 1988).

72 Again, see Floyd, *Is Political Philosophy Impossible?*

73 A. Przeworski, 'Democracy as an equilibrium',
*Public Choice* 123 (2005): 253–73.

74 J. A. Goldstone, R. H. Bates, T. R. Gurr, M. Lustik,
M. G. Marshall, J. Ulfelder, and M. Woodward,
'A global forecasting model of political instabil-
ity', paper presented at the Annual Meeting of the
American Political Science Association, Washington,
DC, 1–4 September 2005, p. 2.

75 R. Wilkinson and K. Pickett, *The Spirit Level: Why
More Equal Societies Almost Always Do Better*
(London: Allen Lane, 2009).

**Chapter 4 Why?**

1 I mention this example, at least in part, because it's
a fairly famous argument by a very famous (at least
within philosophy) political philosopher (though he
is only in part a *political* philosopher). See T. Nagel,
'What is it like to be a bat?', *Philosophical Review*
83/4 (1974): 435–50.

2 M. Nussbaum, The monarchy of fear', www.you
tube.com/watch?v=rKPlhUuoT94.

3 A. Gutmann and D. Thompson, *The Spirit of
Compromise: Why Governing Demands It and
Campaigning Undermines It* (Princeton, NJ:
Princeton University Press, 2014).

4 M. Sandel, 'The moral side of murder', www.you
tube.com/watch?v=kBdfcR-8hEY.
5 'Sen, key contributor to the Human Development
Report, awarded U.S. Humanities Medal', 14
February 2012, www.undp.org/content/undp/en/
home/presscenter/articles/2012/02/14/sen-key-con
tributor-to-the-human-development-report-award
ed-u-s-humanities-medal.html.
6 Cited in A. Przeworski, 'Minimalist conception of
democracy: a defense', in I. Shapiro and C. Hacker-
Cordón (eds), *Democracy's Value* (Cambridge:
Cambridge University Press, 1999), p. 49.
7 For proper discussion of the applicability of
Condorcet's jury theorem to democratic decisions,
see C. List and R. E. Goodin, 'Epistemic democracy:
generalizing the Condorcet jury theorem', *Journal of
Political Philosophy* 9/3 (2001): 277–306.
8 See J. Waldron, *The Harm in Hate Speech*
(Cambridge, MA: Harvard University Press,
2012).
9 For a good account of Cicero's political philosophy, see this chapter by the first person to teach
me anything about Cicero: J. Zetzel, 'Political philosophy', in *The Cambridge Companion to Cicero*
(Cambridge: Cambridge University Press, 2013), pp.
181–95.
10 Cicero, *Political Speeches* (Oxford: Oxford
University Press, 2009).
11 Notably, we also see Aristotle's influence in the
medieval Christian world via Thomas Aquinas
and in the Islamic world via Ibn Khaldun – the
Islamic world being especially important in terms
of preserving and commenting on the Greco-Roman

inheritance, without which Aquinas would not have had his texts at all.

12 Of course, the American republic was not *that* vast at its birth, comprised as it was of a set of former British colonies on the Atlantic seaboard – hence my saying 'the start of something larger' here. As with the Roman Republic, it later grew into something the size of an empire.

13 J. L. Martí and P. Pettit, *A Political Philosophy in Public Life: Civic Republicanism in Zapatero's Spain* (Princeton, NJ: Princeton University Press, 2012).

14 See I. Berlin, *Freedom and its Betrayal* (London: Pimlico Press, 2003), esp. pp. 27–49.

15 See K. Marx, 'Theses on Feuerbach', in G. McLellan (ed.), *Karl Marx: Selected Writings* (Oxford: Oxford University Press, 2000), pp. 171–4.

16 J. S. Hacker, 'The institutional foundations of middle-class democracy', www.policy-network.net/pno_detail.aspx?ID=3998&title=The-institutional-foundations-of-middle-class-democracy.

17 See M. O'Neill and T. Williamson, 'The promise of pre-distribution', www.policy-network.net/pno_detail.aspx?ID=4262&title=The+promise+of+pre-distribution.

18 See www.bsg.ox.ac.uk/faculty-spotlight-jonathan-wolff. Wolff's thoughts on what happens when ethical principles meet concrete policy decisions are also well worth looking at. See J. Wolff, *Ethics and Public Policy: A Philosophical Inquiry* (Abingdon: Routledge, 2011).

19 See www.parliament.uk/biographies/lords/baroness-0%27neill-of-bengarve/2441.

20 See www.parliament.uk/biographies/lords/lord-par ekh/2545.

21 Following up on an earlier theme, Crick also happened to be both a 'republican' and a Machiavelli scholar. See B. Crick, *In Defence of Politics* (London: Continuum, 2005); but also his edition of N. Machiavelli, *The Discourses* (London: Penguin, 2013). Admittedly, the citizenship curriculum has become a much smaller part of a typical child's education than it once was.

22 See A. Beckett, 'PPE: the Oxford degree that runs Britain', *The Guardian*, 23 February 2017, www. theguardian.com/education/2017/feb/23/ppe-oxfo rd-university-degree-that-rules-britain.

23 J. M. Keynes, *The General Theory of Employment, Interest and Money* (London: Wordsworth, 2017), ch. 24.

24 C. Gregoire, 'The unexpected way philosophy majors are changing the world of business', *Huffington Post*, 12 June 2017, www.huffingtonpost.co.uk/entry/why-philosophy-majors-rule_n_4891404?guccounter=1. See also E. Tenner, 'Is philosophy the most practical major?', *The Atlantic*, 16 October 2011, www. theatlantic.com/technology/archive/2011/10/is-phil osophy-the-most-practical-major/246763/.

25 Similarly, how can we be sure that a background in political philosophy would redeem some of the flaws of the new 'tech elite'? See J. Naughton, 'How a half-educated tech elite delivered us into chaos', *The Guardian*, 19 November 2017, www.theguardian. com/commentisfree/2017/nov/19/how-tech-leaders-delivered-us-into-evil-john-naughton.

26 'Why philosophy matters', *IAI News*, 16 November

2017, https://iainews.iai.tv/articles/why-philosophy-matters-auid-973. For more attempts, see J. Weinberg, 'Why is philosophy important?', *Daily Nous*, 8 August 2018, http://dailynous.com/2018/08/08/why-is-philosophy-important/#comment-148363. For debate, R. Scruton and T. Williamson, 'But is it science?', *Times Literary Supplement*, 1 November 2017, see www.the-tls.co.uk/articles/public/roger-scruton-timothy-williamson-philosophy/.

27 'Can an employer demand that you go to work naked?', *BBC News*, 6 December 2017, www.bbc.co.uk/news/stories-42236608.

28 C. Pollard, 'The philosopher who was too hot for Playboy', *The Conversation*, 3 October 2017, https://theconversation.com/the-philosopher-who-was-too-hot-for-playboy-85002.

29 C. Buckley, 'Xi Jinping thought explained: a new ideology for a new era', *New York Times*, www.nytimes.com/2018/02/26/world/asia/xi-jinping-thought-explained-a-new-ideology-for-a-new-era.html.

30 Beckett, 'PPE: the Oxford degree that runs Britain'.

31 C. Brooke, 'Doctors in the house', 28 August 2016, http://virtualstoa.net/2016/08/28/doctors-in-the-house/, and 'Doctors in the house, again', 17 August 2017, http://virtualstoa.net/2017/08/17/doctors-in-the-house-again/. Note, this list is of current or recent MPs with doctorates, most of which are non-philosophical. Nonetheless, there are philosophical or near-philosophical examples here, including Tristram Hunt, Kwasi Kwarteng, Jesse Norman, and Jon Cruddas.

32 M. Desai, 'LSE is paying a heavy price for Saif

Gaddafi's PhD', *The Guardian*, 4 March 2011, www.theguardian.com/commentisfree/2011/mar/04/lse-heavy-price-saif-gaddafis-phd.

33 Actually, the very first airing I gave to this idea can be found in J. Floyd, 'Why we need to teach political philosophy in schools', *The Conversation*, 13 June 2016, http://theconversation.com/why-we-need-to-teach-political-philosophy-in-schools-57749.

34 A. Marr, *The History of Modern Britain* (London: Pan Books, 2017), pp. 163–5.

35 N. Mclean, *Democracy in Chains: The Deep History of the Radical Right's Stealth Plan for America* (London: Penguin, 2017). For comment and summary, see also G. Monbiot, 'A despot in disguise: one man's mission to rip up democracy, *The Guardian*, 19 July 2017, www.theguardian.com/commentisfree/2017/jul/19/despot-disguise-democracy-james-mcgill-buchanan-totalitarian-capitalism?

# Index

# Index

# Index

# Index

# Index